Steak

PRICE: £
DATE: 31/03/15

jacqui
small

Steak

From T-bone steak to Thai beef salad

PAUL GAYLER

Photography by Peter Cassidy

First published in 2006 by Jacqui Small,
an imprint of Aurum Press Ltd,
25 Bedford Avenue, London WC1B 3AT

Publisher Jacqui Small
Editor Madeline Weston
Art Director Lawrence Morton
Food stylist Linda Tubby
Props stylist Roisin Nield
Production Peter Colley

A catalogue record for this book is
available from the British Library.

ISBN 1 903221 42 0

2008   2007   2006

10 9 8 7 6 5 4 3 2 1

Printed and bound in Singapore.

Contents

INTRODUCTION

Ask me and many other chefs what we like to eat on our night off and you may be surprised to hear the response. Working the long hours we do, and cooking so many different and complex dishes, we often crave something simple, quick and easy to prepare. Enter STEAK – it fits the bill perfectly.

There is nothing quite as satisfying as a thick, juicy, good-quality steak, simply grilled over hot coals – ask any barbecue enthusiast. Before you cook a steak, it's important to understand what constitutes a good piece of beef.

This book sets out to give you confidence when cooking steak, with guidance on choosing, storage, preparation, and cooking. The recipes offer a vast range of possibilities: roasting steak joints; savoury grills; delicious sautés and other inspirational dishes. Each recipe recommends the best cuts for perfect results. Understanding these different cuts will enable you to seek out better-quality meat and choose correctly every time.

Good eating!

Paul

What makes a good steak

Most beef produced in the world is graded for quality, usually by government agencies, which is considered vital for their beef industries. The UK and Ireland have set quality assurance schemes to set standards. Generally, grading beef is based on two major factors: the animal's maturity and its fat content. Fat content is vitally important in good beef. The intramuscular fat is integrated with the lean meat, producing an effect called 'marbling'. This inner fat helps keep meat juicy and moist during cooking, producing the best flavour.

The quality of the beef is also greatly improved by hanging. Hanging meat carcasses is known as dry ageing; while the meat is hung in chillers at 1–4°C a hard crust forms on the exterior, and muscle fibre and tissue break down on the inside. As with game, this makes the meat more tender and improves eating quality.

Selecting quality

If you want to buy good-quality meat, you have to be choosy about its provenance. The best beef comes from grass- and grain-fed cattle that are slaughtered when they are at least 24 months old. My favourite beef is British and Irish. The pedigree of both is undeniable.

Here are specific points to look out for when purchasing:

Choose

• Fresh meat, well chilled, from a reputable butcher
• Deep-red, firm-textured flesh with a covering of creamy yellow fat
• Prime joints, such as sirloin, rump and ribs, should be well flecked with inner fat (marbling): remember fat equals flavour
• If buying pre-packed meats look carefully at the labelling, checking for British or Irish meat, and preferably a sign of quality, such as the Soil Association logo, which assures quality and good animal welfare.

Avoid

• Buying cheap meat or frozen meat
• Pale meat with pale white fat, which indicates only minimal ageing
• Pre-packed meat with excess moisture in the tray.

Storing meat

Ideally, meat should be stored at 1–4°C. Remember to remove it from the fridge and allow it to stand at room temperature for 30 minutes before cooking. Keep raw meat away from cooked food, storing it in a covered container or tray to avoid spillage or seepage.

If you have to freeze meat for one reason or another (which I generally do not advocate), ensure it is well wrapped and frozen as quickly as possible. Use it within three months of freezing.

Choosing the right cuts

Regardless of the quality of the meat, a carcass will have both tough and tender cuts, depending on where they come from; meat is no more than muscle. Some cuts consist of a single muscle – for example, the fillet – while others may be a section of several muscles.

Meat from a part of the animal that is fairly inactive will be more expensive and easier to cook. Cuts taken from the more active joints, such as leg, will have coarser fibres and will need to be cooked slowly.

Leaner cuts of steak rarely hold the best flavour – it is the fattier cuts infused with internal fats (marbling) that give the best flavour.

In the quest for steak that will melt in your mouth, we also have to search out the right cut for a specific cooking method.

Here is a guide to the more common cuts available:

Fore rib, wing rib

Fore rib is the best joint for roasting, to my mind. It has great flavour and texture, good marbling and tenderness. The ribs are cut short for roasting. From this cut the popular **rib eye** (no bone) and **rib steak** (bone on) are taken. Wing rib has a closer texture than the fore rib, but again is superb for roasting, full of flavour and usually very tender. Generally rib steaks are best not marinated before cooking.

Rib steak

Rib steaks are cut from the ribs between the bones, leaving the bone attached or cut into rib-eye steaks. On the bone, the steaks, weighing almost 1 kilo, are generally sliced for two servings. They are full of flavour, with good marbling which keeps them succulent.
Rib-eye steak These steaks are prepared from a boneless rolled rib, and are served as single portions, about 280g in weight.

Sirloin and sirloin steak

The sirloin is found between the ribs and the rump. A boneless sirloin is often known as a **strip loin**. They make excellent roasting joints as well as very tasty steaks cut across the grain. Sirloin steaks have a firm texture and lots of flavour. They are usually cut 2–2.5cm thick. Often known as **entrecôte steaks**, they are great for grilling.
Minute steak This is a small sliced sirloin steak about 5mm–1cm thick. It needs to be quickly seared for the best results..
Porterhouse steak It is cut from the rib end of the sirloin, usually about 5cm thick, weighing about 400g as a single serving. Only 2–3 porterhouse steaks can be obtained from one joint.

Fillet and fillet steak

Fillet is the muscle housed on the underside of the rump and sirloin. It is the most tender part of the entire animal. The fillet can be roasted whole, then sliced to make a lovely presentation. It is also used whole in beef Wellington, and can be used in other dishes which need extremely tender meat, such as carpaccio and beef tartare. Trimmed, it produces a beautiful fillet steak, weighing on average 175–225g, that the French give different names to – filet mignon, tournedos, Chateaubriand etc. It does require careful cooking, as it can be dry.
Filet mignon steak Filet mignon (or little steak) is a thinner-cut steak from the narrow tail end of the fillet. It is very tender but, like all cuts from the fillet, requires care and attention when cooking.
Tournedos steak Similar to fillet steak but generally cut closer to the head of the whole fillet. It can be cut in various sizes, as desired.
Chateaubriand The name for the cut taken from the head of the whole long fillet, usually roasted or grilled whole for two people, often served with béarnaise sauce.

T-bone steak

T-bone steak is cut from the chump end of the sirloin. It is easily identified by its 'T'-shaped bone, which has both sirloin and fillet steak attached.

Rump steak

A flavourful steak but it can be a little tough in texture, slightly chewy. It needs to be cooked with care. It can be used as a secondary roasting joint – ask your butcher for top rump. Rump also braises well when used in slow-cooked dishes.

Topside

A joint taken from the inside of the hind legs. It is usually left whole and used as a roast which needs to be well cooked and well rested, then thinly sliced. It can be dry, as there is less marbling so butchers often wrap it in fat which bastes it as it cooks. Topside cut into steaks is more often braised, cooked slowly at a low temperature until meltingly tender.

Chuck/blade

These two joints are taken from the shoulder and neck area of the animal, made up of several muscles. In general they are used only in slow, braised dishes.

Feather steak

This is a shoulder joint; generally feather steak is used for braised dishes. It has an excellent flavour that improves with long cooking.

While most of the great steaks come from the loin and rib, below are two that are not cut from roasting-style joints.

Flank steak

A lean, flat cut, coarse textured and flavourful. It marinates well for quick grilling, but don't overcook it or it will be tough. Also good stuffed and rolled. It is often known by its French name, *bavette*.

Skirt (or goose skirt) steak

Skirt has a lot of marbled fat, full of pure beef flavour. It is removed in one piece but when trimmed, it can be divided into two pieces. These can be braised, but they also make two great steak pieces, which can be grilled. It's important to cook them rare and slice them thinly for the best results.

Cooking methods

The best beef for roasting or steaks comes from the back half of the animal, and the most tender cuts from parts such as the loin and the ribs. As exercise develops the muscles, cuts from parts such as the lower leg, shoulder and neck, need to be cooked slowly by the moist heat method.

Grilling and barbecuing

Grilling has a well-justified reputation for being fast and healthy. Whether you are using a simple ridged grill pan, a grill or an outdoor barbecue, it requires a little practice, but does give great results.

An overhead domestic grill is not really suitable for cooking steaks, as it generally cannot supply enough heat. Grill pans should be almost smoking before you start to cook, while charcoals should be ash grey. To prevent smoking, always brush the meat with oil rather than the grill. Leaner pieces of meat may need to be marinated to help them cope with the fierce heat and this also adds flavour. Baste often with the marinade as the steaks cook.

The smallest, most tender steaks should be cooked closest to the heat. The thicker the piece of meat, the longer it will take to cook, and the further from the heat it should be. When grilling, meat needs to be browned quickly to seal in the flavour and caramelise the fat.
Good cuts to grill and barbecue Sirloin, rump, fillet, T-bone, porterhouse, rib-eye, rib steaks and other lean, tender cuts. Skirt or flank can be tender when well hung and cooked just to medium rare.

Roasting/pan roasting

Roasting is the cooking of prime cuts by dry heat. The art of roasting is to achieve the perfect balance of taste and succulence. Roasting times (see opposite) are calculated by the weight of the meat and the degree of doneness you require. The prime cuts, such as loin and rump, are best roasted at a high heat, and served rare or medium. Tougher cuts, such as topside and silverside, need thorough cooking to tenderise them and benefit from slow braising.

The oven should always be heated to the correct temperature in advance. Generally small joints are cooked at a high temperature while large joints started at a high temperature, then the heat is reduced to finish the cooking. Meat roasted on the bone tends to be moister, have more flavour and less shrinkage. Boned joints, however, cook more evenly, there is little wastage and they are easier to carve.

Choose a roasting pan suitable for the size of the meat. Too big and the juices will burn; too small or deep and the meat will steam.

Pan roasting describes when smaller joints of meat such as fillet or rib steaks, are quickly seared on all sides in a frying pan, then transferred to the oven. This brings the juices to the surface so that they caramelise, sealing in the flavour and making it look appetising.
Good cuts to roast/pan roast Prime cuts include wing rib, fore rib, sirloin, fillet and rump. Don't be tempted by the appealing look of topside and silverside; keep these for slow pot-roasting or braising.

Frying

Frying or sautéing is a technique of cooking the most tender cuts of meat in a little oil or butter while moving them rapidly in a shallow pan. It is undoubtedly one of the most popular cooking techniques, and stir frying is also another favourite method of quick frying.

The degree of heat is very important – medium-high heat is usually best, as it allows the meat to brown evenly, making it caramelise appetisingly. Too low a heat allows the juices to escape, creating unappetising, half-fried food. Too high a heat and the food will burn before it is cooked inside.

You will need a strong, heavy-bottomed pan for the job. Black cast-iron is popular in the professional kitchen, although nowadays chefs like to use non-stick pans too, ideal for making sauces from the pan juices after frying.

Choose a frying pan suitable for the size of the joint. Do not crowd the pan, as this creates unwanted steam. If you have large amounts of meat to cook, it is best to fry it in batches, but ensure you reheat the pan thoroughly before continuing with the second batch.
Best cuts for frying Tender cuts e.g. fillet, sirloin, rump and rib eye.

Braising

Braising is a method of cooking by moist heat and is ideal for the tougher cuts of steak. These cuts score top marks for taste but need long, slow cooking at low temperature to transform them into memorable meals.

Generally the meat is seared first to caramelise the surface, giving it an appealing colour before it is cooked slowly in a well-flavoured cooking liquid. Cooking times are dictated by the quality of the meat.

Most braising is done in the oven but it can be done on top of the stove, too, as long as it is done gently. Many braised dishes are all the better for being made in advance and reheated thoroughly before serving. Often meat for braising is marinated first in wine with aromatics, which add flavours, and the wine acts as a tenderiser. I suggest investing in a thick cast-iron casserole with a tight-fitting lid, which will conduct the heat well, and distribute it evenly.
Good cuts to braise Topside, silverside and top rump. Also, neck, clod, chuck, blade, thick rib, flank, skirt, shin and leg.

How do you like it cooked?

Cooking steak perfectly can intimidate home cooks, but it really isn't that difficult. The problem is finding out when it is done as you like it.

Different joints and cuts cook at different rates and every one has to be judged for its thickness, internal temperature and fat content. Then there is the question of the temperature of your oven or grill. They can vary immensely, and you have to know your own oven.

Below are some guidelines for perfect results every time.

Roasting (cooked at 190°C) on the bone
Rare 20 minutes per 450g (plus 20 minutes) 60°C*
Medium 25 minutes per 450g (plus 25 minutes) 70°C*
Well done 30 minutes per 450g (plus 30 minutes) 82°C*
final temperature after resting
- For meat roasted off the bone, allow 5 minutes less per 450g (plus 5 minutes less too)
- A roast is best rested for 10–15 minutes before serving

Grilling, frying
The cooking time for steaks will vary with the heat of the grill, the type of pan, the distance of the food from the heat and, of course, the thickness of the meat.

The table below is based on a steak 2.5cm thick, grilled over a high heat. It is best to sear the steak on each side first to caramelise the juices, then cook it to your liking.

Resting meat

Leaving meat to rest after cooking (covered with foil in a warm place) is as important as the cooking itself. During cooking, the heat penetrates from the outside, and at higher temperatures the juices nearest the surface of the meat are forced out. Resting it allows it to cool and continue to cook with the heat that has built up in the meat. The contracted fibres gradually 'relax', allowing the inner juices to coagulate evenly throughout the meat, resulting in a more tender texture and a better taste.

It takes almost the same time to cook a rare steak as it does a well done one because, since the rare steak has minimal cooking, the resting period will be longer.

Some important do's and don'ts when cooking steak

- Season meat just before cooking, or immediately after. If meat is salted too early, the juices are drawn out making the meat dry
- Ensure excess marinade is shaken off meat before grilling
- Never cook steak from frozen, it will be tough. Always leave meat to thaw thoroughly and come to room temperature before cooking
- Never cut a piece of steak off just to see if it's done; flavourful juices will be lost
- Never turn steaks over with a fork as it releases the juices; always turn them with kitchen tongs
- When in doubt, undercook steak rather than ruin it by overcooking.

Cooking degree	Cooking time	Internal temperature	Resting time before serving
Blue Almost raw inside, but hot	1–2 minutes each side	49–52°C	9 minutes
Rare Red inside with plenty of red juices running freely	2–3 minutes each side	58–60°C	8 minutes
Medium rare As rare, but with few free-flowing juices, paler centre	3–4 minutes each side	60–63°C	7 minutes
Medium Pink in the centre with juices set	4–5 minutes each side	65–68°C	6 minutes
Medium well Deep pink in the centre, juices set	5–6 minutes each side	65–70°C	5 minutes
Well done The centre brown but flesh still clear and juicy	6–7 minutes each side	70–77°C	4 minutes
Very well done Centre beige, not many juices remaining	7–8 minutes each side	80–82°C	3 minutes

The ultimate steak and chips

The ultimate steak and chips

Simply grilled steak of any cut is one of the favourite ways to enjoy good beef. The cut depends entirely on your choice, whether tender cuts of fillet, tournedos, T-bone or more highly flavoured ones like sirloin steak, rib-eye etc. For cooking the ultimate steak see page 9. With the steak, I like to serve a simple grill garnish and the best quality accompaniment of good chips. Sauce béarnaise is my favourite sauce, although any of the cold butters is excellent.

SERVES 4

4 flat mushrooms, trimmed and cleaned

little olive oil

1 garlic clove, thinly sliced

1 sprig thyme

4 tomatoes

4 x your chosen steak (sirloin, rib-eye,
    fillet, T-bone, porterhouse, flank)

100g watercress (optional)

your favourite sauce, béarnaise or
    flavoured butters (see pages 133)

FOR THE CHIPS

1.2kg floury potatoes (such as maris
    piper), peeled

sunflower oil for deep frying

coarse sea salt

1. Place the mushrooms in a small dish with the olive oil, garlic, thyme and leave to marinate for 1 hour.
2. To make the chips, trim the potatoes then cut them into sticks about 1 x 7.5cm. Keep in cold water until needed, then drain and dry in a clean cloth.
3. Heat the sunflower oil slowly to 160°C and cook the chips in the oil to blanch them for 4–6 minutes with no colour; remove and drain them. Increase the oil temperature to 190°C, return the chips to the pan and fry until golden and crisp. Drain on kitchen paper.
4. Grill the mushrooms and tomatoes on the grill while cooking the steak to your liking. Garnish the steaks with the mushrooms, tomatoes, watercress, if using, and the sauce of your choice. Serve with the chips, sprinkled with coarse salt.

Grilled fillet Niçoise, olive béarnaise

What I love about béarnaise sauce is its versatility. Here it is flavoured with black olives, giving it a nuance of Provence: an altogether healthy and wonderful tasting dish.

SERVES 4

4 tbsp olive oil

1 garlic clove, sliced

sprig of fresh thyme plus extra to garnish

6 fresh basil leaves

4 x 180g fillet steaks

2 courgettes, cut lengthways into
    3mm thick slices

1 aubergine, cut into 5mm slices

1 red pepper, skinned, halved, deseeded,
    cut into strips

2 tomatoes, skinned, halved, deseeded

2 tbsp balsamic vinegar

FOR THE OLIVE BÉARNAISE

1 tbsp chopped black olives

150ml béarnaise sauce (see page 133)

salt and freshly cracked black pepper

1. Mix all the olive oil with the garlic and herbs in a dish. Add the meat and coat well with the marinade. Cover with clingfilm, marinate at room temperature for 4 hours.
2. Remove the meat, add the vegetables and the tomatoes to the oil, and marinate for a further 2 hours.
3. Heat a pan grill and, when hot, heat a little of the marinade in the pan, place the vegetables and beef on the grill until the vegetables are golden and lightly charred all over. Grill the beef to your liking.
4. Mix the olives with the prepared béarnaise sauce, and season to taste.
5. Arrange the grilled vegetables on plates and sprinkle the balsamic vinegar over. Arrange the beef on top of the vegetables and spoon a little olive béarnaise over each steak. Garnish with thyme and serve.

Grilled fillet Niçoise, olive béarnaise

Grilled teriyaki steak
with grilled beans, chilli and shallots

When you are feeling like something a little different, but at the same time simple, this Japanese steak preparation fits the bill beautifully.

SERVES 4

8 x 90g mignon steaks or skirt steaks
375g French beans
6 large banana shallots, cut into thick
 slices
2 tbsp olive oil
8 spring onions, shredded
1 tbsp fresh picked coriander leaves
2 tbsp hot chilli sauce
salt and freshly cracked black pepper

FOR THE MARINADE

6 tbsp dark soy sauce
2 tsp caster sugar
2 tbsp sake or dry sherry
2 garlic cloves, crushed
5cm piece root ginger, finely grated

1 Prepare the marinade by combining the soy, sugar, sake, garlic and ginger in a large dish. Add the steaks, allow to marinate for 2–3 hours at room temperature, remove, reserving the marinade.
2 Cook the French beans in boiling salted water for 8–10 minutes then drain and refresh them in cold water.
3 Heat a chargrill or pan grill until smoking. Cook the steaks over a high heat until cooked to your liking, golden and charred all over, remove and keep warm.
4 Place the beans in a bowl with the shallots and toss with the oil. Place the beans and shallots on the grill and cook until lightly charred and wilted. Place in a bowl, add the spring onion, coriander and the chilli sauce, lightly toss together and season to taste.
5 Heat the marinade in a pan until boiling. Dress some grilled beans on 4 individual serving plates, top each with 2 grilled teriyaki mignon. Pour the marinade sauce over and serve.

Grilled sirloin steak with thyme potatoes, anchovy–caper dressing

Here is one of the most popular dishes in my steak repertoire. Anchovy and capers have the natural acidity to cut through the richness of a grilled juicy steak. Some grilled asparagus or radicchio is also great served with this dish.

SERVES 4

450g waxy new potatoes, well scrubbed
salt and freshly cracked black pepper
2 tbsp olive oil plus extra for brushing
1 tsp fresh thyme leaves
4 x 200g sirloin steaks, trimmed of fat

FOR THE DRESSING

½ tsp Dijon mustard
1 garlic clove, crushed
1 tbsp white wine vinegar
4 tbsp olive oil
1 shallot, finely chopped
2 tbsp superfine capers, rinsed, dried
2 anchovy fillets, rinsed, dried, chopped
1 hard boiled egg, chopped
½ red pepper, deseeded, cut into 5mm dice

1 Cook the potatoes in a pan of boiling salted water until just tender, then drain, cut in half lengthways. Place in a dish, toss with the olive oil and thyme, along with a little seasoning.
2 Make the dressing, place the mustard, garlic and wine vinegar in a bowl, whisk in the olive oil to form a dressing. Add the remaining ingredients, toss well together, season to taste, place to one side.
3 Heat a ridged pan grill or preferably a barbecue until smoking, then add the potatoes and cook until golden on both sides, about 10–12 minutes, remove and keep warm.
4 Wipe the pan grill clean. Brush the steaks with a little more oil and season with salt and pepper. Grill as desired, about 5–6 minutes per side for medium rare.
5 Heat the prepared dressing over a low heat. Arrange the grilled potatoes on 4 individual serving plates. Slice each steak into 4 thick slices and arrange next to the potatoes. Spoon the warm dressing over and serve.

Irish carpet bag steak

It wasn't until quite recently that I learnt from an Australian chef friend of mine that carpet bag steak originated from Australia and is not an American invention as I had always thought. Could this be the dish that led to the creation of the famous surf and turf concept, who knows? It's a simple dish that relies on the best steak and top quality fresh oysters, which for me, at present, are from Ireland.

SERVES 4

4 x 180g fillet, rump or sirloin steaks
12 medium rock oysters, preferably Irish
salt and freshly cracked black pepper
25g unsalted butter, softened
juice of 2 lemons
2 tbsp Worcester sauce
2 tbsp chopped fresh Italian flat-leaf
   parsley

1 Using a good sharp knife, slit each steak lengthways to form a pocket.
2 Open the oysters, strain and reserve the liquor. Season the oysters and insert 3 into each steak pocket. Close the openings with a small cocktail stick.
3 Heat a pan grill or barbecue until smoking. Season the exterior of the steaks. Add the steaks to the grill and cook to your liking.
4 Meanwhile, mix the oyster liquor, softened butter, lemon juice, Worcester sauce and parsley, spoon over the cooked steaks, then serve. For an oriental variation, add 2 tbsp oyster sauce to the oyster and lemon juices, and pour over the steaks, it is equally delicious.

Grilled sirloin steak
with thyme potatoes,
anchovy–caper dressing

Texas porterhouse steak with spicy chilli salsa and onion rings

Porterhouse steak is one of the greatest tasting steaks. Marinating the meat breaks down the meat fibres, making it more tender and adding depth of flavour. The onion rings are also finished with the same spices.

SERVES 4

2 tsp paprika
½ tsp chilli powder
2 tsp ground coriander
1 tsp salt
1 tsp sugar
½ tsp cracked black pepper
½ tsp dry mustard powder
4 x 350g porterhouse or preferred steaks
4 tbsp olive oil
150ml spicy chilli salsa (see page 142)

FOR THE ONION RINGS

vegetable oil for deep frying
2 tbsp flour
2 onions, peeled, thinly sliced

1 In a dish, mix all the spices with the salt, sugar, pepper and mustard powder. Remove 1 tbsp and reserve for the onions.
2 Take the steaks and bat them well with a kitchen mallet or with a sharp fork. Add to the spices, pour the oil over, and massage the meat with the spice mix. Cover the dish with clingfilm and place in the fridge overnight. Before cooking bring the steaks to room temperature.
3 Heat a pan grill until smoking, remove the steaks from marinade and cook on the grill to your liking.
4 Meanwhile heat the vegetable oil in a deep fat fryer or large pan to 180°C.
5 Mix the flour with the reserved spice mix, then pass the onions through the spiced flour, and carefully drop into the hot oil to fry them for 3–4 minutes or until golden. Remove with a slotted spoon and drain on kitchen paper.
6 Place the cooked steaks on individual plates, top with the spicy chilli salsa and a pile of the onion rings, then serve.

Grilled porterhouse with Argentinean parsley sauce, tomato relish

This parsley sauce is known as *chimichurri* sauce in Latin America. It is a flavour-packed and is also great brushed on thick bread for a steak sandwich. For those who love strong flavours, especially garlic, this is your call!

SERVES 4

4 x 475g porterhouse (T-bone) steaks,
  2.5cm thick
2 tbsp olive oil
salt and freshly cracked black pepper

FOR THE SAUCE

small bunch fresh Italian flat-leaf parsley
4 large garlic cloves, crushed
100ml olive oil
4 tbsp white wine vinegar
1 tbsp fresh oregano leaves
½ tsp crushed red chilli flakes

FOR THE RELISH

75g dark brown sugar
175g sunblush tomatoes, chopped
1 onion, finely chopped
4 tbsp balsamic vinegar
1 tsp tomato purée
1 tsp mustard powder
1 tsp ground cumin

1 To prepare the relish, place the sugar with 120ml of water over a low heat, bring to the boil until the sugar dissolves. Add the tomatoes, onion, vinegar, tomato purée and mustard, and simmer gently together for 25 minutes until the relish becomes thick and slightly caramelised in flavour. Season with salt and pepper and cumin, leave to cool.
2 Make the parsley sauce. Strip the parsley leaves from the stems and discard the stems. Place the parsley leaves and garlic in a food processor and coarsely process them. Pour the olive oil, white vinegar and 3 tbsp water through the feeder tube at the top, whiz again.
3 Finally, add the oregano and chilli, along with a little salt and pepper and give it one final whiz until blended.
4 Heat a chargrill or pan grill until smoking, brush the steaks with olive oil all over and season with salt and pepper. Cook the steaks to your liking, and place on individual serving plates with the tomato relish alongside. Pour the parsley sauce over the steaks and serve.

Texas porterhouse steak with spicy chilli salsa and onion rings

Wood-grilled T-bone steak Florentina style

Wood-grilled steaks are utterly delicious, the wood imparting a delicate flavour and aroma to the meat. In Italy, T-bone steaks are the authentic cut of meat used for this dish, topped with a flavour-packed oil of garlic and herbs. If you prefer, any cut of steak could be prepared the same way. If you do not have the option of using a wood grill, a plain charcoal or small pan grill would be fine but of course would not give the same result.

SERVES 4
4 x 475g T-bone steaks
salt and freshly cracked black pepper

FOR THE SAUCE
40g picked fresh rosemary
40g fresh basil
125ml extra-virgin olive oil
3 garlic cloves, crushed

1 Heat a barbecue with a mixture of charcoal and wood (ideally mesquite) until very hot and the flames have died down ready for grilling.
2 Make the sauce. Place the herbs, oil and garlic in a blender or food processor and whiz until they have a coarse texture.
3 Season the T-bone steaks well, then place on the prepared grill. Baste regularly with the herb–oil sauce as they cook to your desired liking.
4 Drizzle the steaks with any remaining herb oil before serving. I love to serve this dish with some simple grilled new potatoes and grilled peppers.

T-bone steak with sour cream, wasabi dressing

This is a simple recipe – ready in minutes. Wasabi paste or Japanese horseradish is available from oriental stores.

SERVES 4

4 x 450–550g T-bone steaks, about
  2cm thick
3 tbsp light soy sauce
2 tbsp olive oil
2 tbsp chopped fresh coriander
2.5cm piece root ginger, grated
1 tbsp brown sugar
1 tbsp mirin or dry sherry

1 Place the steaks in a large dish. Mix together the soy sauce, olive oil, coriander, ginger, sugar and mirin, pour over the steaks, cover, and leave to marinate for 1 hour at room temperature, turning them occasionally.
2 For the dressing (see below), mix all the ingredients together in a bowl and chill in the fridge until needed.
3 Grill the steaks in normal manner to your liking, and serve with the wasabi dressing.

FOR THE DRESSING
150ml sour cream
½ tsp wasabi paste
3 spring onions, finely chopped

FOR THE TAPENADE
25g green olives, stoned
30g superfine capers, rinsed
2 garlic cloves, crushed
3 tbsp olive oil
100g sunblush tomatoes in oil
1 tbsp lemon juice
1 tsp fresh rosemary
salt and freshly cracked black pepper

T-bone steak with rosemary and sunblush tapenade

This tapenade makes a great dip for cheese straws or for spreading on bread drizzled with olive oil.

SERVES 4

4 x 350g T-bone steaks, about 2cm thick
2 sprigs fresh rosemary
2 tbsp olive oil

1 Using a small knife, cut slits into the flesh of the steaks. Break the rosemary into needles, then stud them into the slits, place in a dish, pour the olive oil over, cover and marinate at room temperature for 2 hours.

2 Meanwhile make the tapenade (see left) by placing the olives and capers along with the garlic and olive oil in a blender and process to a coarse paste. Add the sunblush tomatoes and their oil, the lemon juice and rosemary and whiz again. Season to taste.

3 Grill the T-bone steaks in the normal manner to your liking, top with the sunblush tapenade and serve. Some sour-cream topped baked potatoes would make a great accompaniment.

Steak on toast with barbecued devilled oysters

You may be surprised to see HP sauce being used in this recipe, but don't be. It works wonders for this simple devilled barbecue sauce. I'm a great advocate of using ketchup and prepared relishes if the quality is good.

SERVES 4

2 tbsp sunflower oil

1 onion, finely sliced

1 tbsp chopped fresh coriander

salt and freshly cracked black pepper

4 x 175g fillet or rump steaks

8 oysters

8 rashers streaky bacon or pancetta

4 thick slices good quality white bread

2 beefsteak tomatoes, each thinly sliced
  into 4 slices

1 For the barbecue sauce, heat the oil in a pan, add the garlic and onion and cook for 2–3 minutes until the onion is soft and tender. Add the remaining ingredients. Gently bring to the boil and simmer for 10 minutes, stirring occasionally. Keep the sauce warm.

2 Heat 1 tbsp of the sunflower oil in a frying pan, add the onion and cook until golden, about 5–6 minutes; add the chopped coriander, season to taste and keep warm.

3 Heat a pan grill until smoking, season the steaks with salt and pepper. Wrap each oyster in a slice of bacon and secure with a cocktail stick. Brush the steaks and oysters with oil and grill until the steaks are done to your liking. The oysters will take about 2–3 minutes just until the bacon is browned.

4 Toast the bread on both sides until golden, top with the coriander-flavoured onion, and top each with some sliced tomato.

5 Place a steak and 2 grilled oysters in bacon on each toast, pour some barbecue sauce over and serve immediately.

FOR THE BARBECUE SAUCE

1 tbsp olive oil

2 garlic cloves, crushed

1 onion, finely chopped

100ml HP brown sauce

1 tbsp brown sugar

1 tsp Dijon mustard

½ tsp red chilli flakes

salt and pinch of cayenne

Steak sandwich with Virgin Mary tomato relish

A hearty steak sandwich to brighten up the most jaded of palates. Packed with flavour, the spicy yoghurt mix gives the steaks a melting tenderness. If smoked paprika is not easily available, simply replace it with a sweet variety.

SERVES 4

100ml plain yoghurt
generous pinch of sugar
1 garlic clove, crushed
1 tsp tomato purée
1 tsp smoked paprika
1 tsp ground cumin
4 x 150g rump steaks,
    trimmed of all fat
olive oil for cooking
salt and freshly
    cracked black pepper

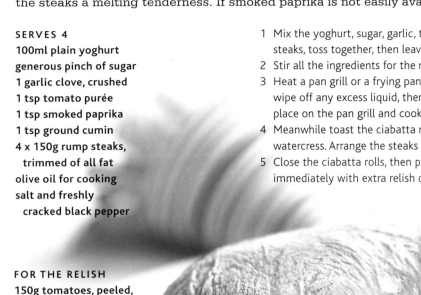

FOR THE RELISH

150g tomatoes, peeled,
    deseeded, finely
    chopped
2 tbsp creamed
    horseradish
1 tbsp chopped
    fresh cilantro
1 tsp hot pepper
    sauce
½ tsp Worcester
    sauce

1 Mix the yoghurt, sugar, garlic, tomato purée, paprika and cumin together in a bowl. Add the steaks, toss together, then leave to marinate for up to 1 hour at room temperature.

2 Stir all the ingredients for the relish together in a bowl, season to taste.

3 Heat a pan grill or a frying pan until very hot. Remove the steaks from their marinade and wipe off any excess liquid, then brush them lightly with oil. Season the steaks well, then place on the pan grill and cook to your liking.

4 Meanwhile toast the ciabatta rolls, then top the bases with onion, cucumber and watercress. Arrange the steaks on top, followed by a generous dollop of relish.

5 Close the ciabatta rolls, then press down lightly. Cut each one in half then serve immediately with extra relish on the side. Serve with some crispy French fries.

TO SERVE

4 ciabatta rolls, split
1 small red onion, thinly sliced
¼ cucumber, thinly sliced
50g watercress

Adobado grilled rib-eye steak

Adobo is a Mexican spice composed of dried chilli, spices and vinegar – it packs a heady punch and lovers of spice will be enthralled by this dish. Dishes like this prepared *en Adobado* refer to the way the meat is grilled or roasted in a thick coating of the marinade. I like to serve this with the sweet, cool tasting Blood orange and avocado salsa (see page 142). Using a chargrill is the best way to enjoy these steaks.

SERVES 4
salt and freshly cracked black pepper
½ tsp Dijon mustard
4 x 275g rib-eye steaks
2 dried red chillies, preferably ancho chillies
2 garlic cloves, crushed
1 onion, finely chopped
¼ tsp ground cumin
¼ tsp dried oregano
25g unsalted butter
1 tbsp sundried tomato purée
1 tsp red wine or balsamic vinegar
Blood orange and avocado salsa (see page 142)

1 Mix 1 tsp of salt, ½ tsp cracked black pepper and the mustard and rub all over the rib-eye steaks; place in a dish and leave to stand for 30 minutes.

2 Heat a heavy-based frying pan on the heat, add the dried chillies and dry toast them for 2–3 minutes, keeping them moving in the pan. Transfer to a bowl, cover with boiling water for 15 minutes, then drain them, discarding the water.

3 Transfer the chillies to a blender, add 125ml water and process to a purée. Add the garlic, onion, cumin, oregano and whiz again, remove and set aside.

4 Melt the butter in a small pan, add the chilli purée and cook over a high heat, stirring constantly, for 3–4 minutes.

5 Add the tomato purée, cook for a further 2 minutes. Add the vinegar, cook over low heat until the sauce thickens, about 20 minutes. Cover the rib-eye steaks with the sauce and marinate up to 1 hour at room temperature.

6 Preheat a barbecue grill or pan grill until smoking, place the steaks on it, still coated in the chilli marinade sauce, and cook to your liking, turning often so that they don't burn. Serve thinly sliced or whole with the blood orange and avocado salsa.

Rib-eye steak, Camembert à l'escargot

I first prepared this dish when a young lad and I was entering every culinary competition in the country – and abroad – whenever possible. This dish won me one such cheese competition to my great pleasure and I include it here for sentimental reasons and because it is a great dish of which I am proud!

SERVES 4

4 x 200g rib-eye steaks or rump, 5mm thick
salt and freshly cracked black pepper
1 tbsp olive oil
4 x half thick wedges of Camembert cheese at room temperature

FOR THE SAUCE

30g unsalted butter
1 garlic clove, crushed
75g canned snails, drained
50g Parma ham, finely chopped
2 shallots, finely chopped
2 tbsp dry white wine
150ml well-flavoured beef stock (see page 141)
1 tbsp chopped fresh Italian flat-leaf parsley

1 Preheat the oven to 150°C. Heat a pan grill until very hot, season the steaks well with salt and pepper and brush them with the olive oil.
2 Place the steaks on the grill, cook to your liking until golden and crusty all over. Top each steak with a wedge of Camembert and keep warm in the oven.
3 For the sauce, heat half the butter in a frying pan, add the garlic and cook for 2–3 minutes. Increase the heat, add the snails, Parma ham and shallots, and sauté for 1 minute. Pour the wine over and boil for 1 minute. Add the stock and simmer until the sauce is reduced by half. Whisk in the remaining butter, add the parsley and season to taste.
4 Arrange the cheese-topped steaks on serving plates, spoon the snail sauce over and serve.

Grilled rib-eye with salsa verde on cracked wheat *panzanella*

The salsa verde makes plenty; it will keep covered in the fridge for 2–3 days and is good served with pasta or grilled chicken. In the *panzanella*, a staple of Tuscan cuisine, I replace the normal bread with a soaked cracked wheat.

SERVES 4

4 x 180g rib-eye steaks
2 tbsp olive oil

FOR THE SALSA VERDE

40g Dijon mustard
100ml olive oil
50g fresh basil
25g young spinach leaves, stalks removed
20g superfine capers
2 anchovy fillets, rinsed
2 garlic cloves, crushed

1 To make the salsa, place the mustard in a small bowl and slowly whisk in the olive oil. Place in a liquidiser, add all the remaining ingredients, purée finely, and season to taste with salt and freshly cracked black pepper; place on one side.

2 For the *panzanella*, place the cracked wheat in a bowl, just cover with boiling water, cover with clingfilm and leave for 30 minutes to swell up and until all the water has been absorbed. Fluff up with a fork. Add the remaining ingredients and toss well together. Season to taste and leave for 20 minutes to allow the flavours to blend.

3 Heat a chargrill or pan grill until smoking. Brush the steaks with the olive oil and season with salt and pepper. Grill to your liking, until tender and well browned.

4 Arrange the *panzanella* on 4 serving plates. Serve the steaks, sliced or whole, on top of the *panzanella* and spoon the salsa verde over.

FOR THE *PANZANELLA*
120g cracked wheat (bulgur)
10 red cherry tomatoes, halved
10 yellow cherry tomatoes, halved
40g black olives, pitted
1 red onion, chopped
2 tbsp red wine vinegar
120ml olive oil

Stuffed rump steak with goat's cheese, black mushrooms, and watercress and almond butter

I love goat's cheese in any form – for this stuffing you will need to source a mature goat's cheese for added flavour. Trompette mushrooms are a wild mushroom variety, with earthy flavours, available in fresh or dried form although any mushroom will work well.

SERVES 4

2 tbsp olive oil

2 shallots, finely chopped

1 garlic clove, crushed

75g trompette mushrooms or flat mushrooms, chopped

100g mature goat's cheese, crumbled

1 tbsp chopped fresh Italian flat-leaf parsley

1 tsp Dijon mustard

75g fresh white breadcrumbs

4 x 180g rump steaks about 4cm thick

120g Watercress and almond butter (see page 137)

1. For the stuffing, heat the olive oil in a frying pan, add the shallots, garlic and chopped mushrooms and cook over a high heat for 5 minutes until the mushrooms are tender. Transfer to a bowl and leave to cool.
2. When cold, add the cheese, parsley, mustard and breadcrumbs and mix together.
3. Make a slit in the side of the steaks to form deep pockets. Push the stuffing well into each pocket and close the opening with a cocktail stick.
4. Cook the steaks on a hot barbecue or pan grill to your liking. Cut the steaks into thick slices and serve topped with slices of the watercress and almond butter.

Mediterranean beef skewers with chickpea purée

Baharat means 'spice' in Arabic: it is a mixed spice that is available from Middle Eastern grocers and its content varies from region to region; it has a rich brown colour and perfume. Pomegranate molasses is also available from Middle Eastern stores, it is thick and syrupy with a distinctive acidity which works well with the sweet apricots.

SERVES 4
2 tbsp olive oil
1 garlic clove, crushed
5cm piece root ginger, finely grated
1 tsp ground cumin
¼ tsp ground turmeric
1 tbsp *baharat* spices
4 tbsp pomegranate molasses
700g skirt steak or rump steak, cut crosswise into 2.5cm pieces
12 dried apricots, soaked in warm water for 30 minutes, drained
small whole fresh mint leaves
4 large pre-soaked wooden skewers

FOR THE CHICKPEA PURÉE
400g cooked fresh or canned chickpeas, drained
1 garlic clove, crushed
100ml full fat milk
juice of ¼ lemon
salt and freshly cracked black pepper
2 tbsp olive oil
1 tsp cumin seeds

1 Heat the olive oil in a pan, add the garlic, ginger, cumin, turmeric and *baharat* spices and cook for 1 minute to infuse the spices. Add the pomegranate molasses and cook for a further minute.
2 Place the beef in a dish, pour the spice mix over and mix well. Leave to go cold, about 1 hour.
3 Remove the meat from marinade, and thread the pieces alternately with the soaked apricots onto the skewers.
4 Heat a ridged grill or barbecue and, when hot, add the pepared skewers and cook for 5–6 minutes, turning them during grilling.
5 Meanwhile, make the chickpea purée: place the chickpeas in a blender with the garlic, milk and lemon juice. Season with salt and pepper and whiz until smooth.
6 Heat the olive oil in a small pan, add the cumin seeds and cook over low heat for 1 minute to infuse the seeds. Add the chickpea purée, mix well and heat through for 2–3 minutes.
7 Serve the grilled skewers with the spiced chickpea purée, sprinkle the mint over and serve.

Green-tea beef kebabs

For me, tea (and for that matter coffee), is one of the most under utilised ingredients in the kitchen, only to appear to provide a soothing cuppa! In cooking, tea has a unique flavour that Far Eastern cultures have admired for centuries.

SERVES 4

600g sirloin beef, cut into 2.5cm pieces

1 large red onion, cut into 8 wedges

2 green peppers, deseeded, cut into large pieces

1 aubergine, cut into large pieces

2 tbsp olive oil

4 large pre-soaked wooden skewers

FOR THE MARINADE

2 tbsp light soy sauce

2 sticks lemongrass, outer casing removed, inner chopped

1 tbsp sweet chilli sauce

1 tsp chilli oil

2 tsp loose green tea or split tea bags

3 garlic cloves, crushed

1cm piece root ginger, grated

25g fresh coriander, roughly chopped

1 Place the beef pieces in a bowl, add the marinade ingredients and mix well to amalgamate all the flavours. Cover with clingfilm and refrigerate for 24 hours to marinate.

2 Remove the beef from the marinade and discard the marinade.

3 Preheat a barbecue or pan grill until smoking. Thread the beef with the vegetable pieces onto the prepared skewers and brush all over with oil.

4 Place the kebabs on the grill, grill for 8–10 minutes or to you liking. I suggest serving the kebabs with stir-fried or steamed rice.

Beef satay, bang bang sauce

A traditional Malay dish with an increasing popularity throughout Britain due to the rise in interest in the cuisine of southeast Asia. Smaller made satays make great canapés served at cocktail parties or with pre-dinner drinks.

SERVES 4

800g sirloin steak, trimmed of all fat

4 sticks lemongrass, outer casing removed, inner chopped

2 tbsp brown sugar

1 tbsp fish sauce (*nam pla*)

1 garlic clove, crushed

2.5cm piece root ginger, chopped

½ tsp coriander seeds

½ tsp cumin seeds

½ tsp ground turmeric

8 pre-soaked wooden or bamboo skewers

oil for brushing

FOR THE SAUCE

300ml well-flavoured chicken stock

6 tbsp smooth peanut butter

2 tbsp brown sugar

1 red chilli, deseeded, finely chopped

2.5cm piece root ginger, finely chopped

1 tsp mild curry powder

1 garlic clove, crushed

½ tsp soy sauce

juice of ½ lemon

1 Cut the steak into 2.5cm long pieces, then place in a large bowl.

2 Place all the remaining ingredients, with 50ml of water, in a blender or food processor and whiz to a wet paste, pour over the meat, and toss together. Cover with clingfilm, then marinate in the fridge overnight.

3 Divide the meat equally and thread onto the 8 skewers, brushing lightly with oil.

4 Heat a barbecue or pan grill until very hot; meanwhile prepare the sauce. Place all the sauce ingredients in a small pan, bring to the boil, reduce the heat, and simmer for 2–3 minutes. Pour into a bowl and leave to cool.

5 Cook the satays on the grill for 3–4 minutes until golden and caramelised all over. Serve the satays with the sauce separately. Some shredded onion and chopped cucumber are the traditional accompaniments.

Steak au poivre

Steak au poivre

The success of this classic French black-pepper beef dish relies on the flavour of the peppercorns, which must be cracked just before needed to release their aroma. This dish dates back to the nineteenth century when pepper was considered an aphrodisiac, but it remains popular to this day. In France it is usually served with sauté potatoes.

SERVES 4

3 tbsp fresh black peppercorns

4 x 180g beef fillet steaks, about 4–5cm thick

salt

2 tbsp clarified butter (see page 44)

100ml cognac or other brandy

150ml well-flavoured beef stock (see page 141)

4 tbsp double cream

100g unsalted butter, chilled, cut in small pieces

1 Place the peppercorns in a folded tea towel, then crush them with a rolling pan or kitchen mallet. They should be broken and coarsely cracked, not ground. Place the cracked peppercorns in a shallow dish and roll the steaks in them until they are evenly coated. Season the steaks with a little salt.

2 Heat the clarified butter in a large non-stick frying pan and, when hot, add the steaks and cook over a high heat until well browned and cooked to your liking. Remove the steaks and keep warm.

3 Add the cognac to the hot pan, then carefully ignite it with a taper. Allow the cognac to burn off, then add the stock and reduce by half.

4 Add the cream and reduce until thick enough to coat the back of a spoon. Whisk in the butter to enrich the sauce and season to taste with a little salt. Pour the sauce over the steaks and serve.

Filet mignons with Marsala-glazed shallots and wild mushrooms

Tender steak cooked with shallots and wild mushrooms is a much loved combination. If fresh wild mushrooms are not available use a selection of dried ones instead. It is important that the sauce has an intense rich flavour.

SERVES 4

2 tbsp clarified butter (see page 44)

8 x 90g filet mignon steaks

salt and freshly cracked black pepper

25g unsalted butter, chilled, cut into small pieces

225g mixed fresh wild mushrooms, sliced

1 garlic clove, crushed

12 medium size banana shallots, peeled, halved lengthways

1 tbsp brown sugar

150ml Marsala

200ml well-flavoured beef stock (see page 141)

1 tsp chopped fresh thyme plus a little to garnish

1 Heat the clarified butter in a non-stick frying pan and, when hot, season the steaks liberally with salt and pepper and add to the pan. Fry the steaks for 2–3 minutes on each side, until browned. Remove and keep warm until ready.

2 Heat 15g of the unsalted butter in the pan and fry the mushrooms with the garlic for 2–3 minutes. Remove from the pan and keep warm.

3 Return the pan to the heat, add the shallots, the sugar and lightly caramelise them together, about 4–5 minutes. Pour the Marsala and stock into the pan and cook for 4–5 minutes or until the shallots are cooked, and the sauce thick and syrupy and reduced by half. Add the mushrooms to the sauce with the chopped thyme, then stir in the remaining unsalted butter to enrich the sauce. Season to taste.

4 Serve the steaks, 2 filet mignons per person, coated with the shallot and mushroom sauce and garnished with thyme. I suggest some creamy mashed potato to accompany this dish.

Filet mignons with Marsala-glazed
shallots and wild mushrooms

Beef tournedos 'venison style' with juniper berries, chestnut blinis

Marinating the beef in red wine and juniper gives it a wonderful flavour with the accent on winter. The chestnut pancakes make a great accompaniment to the beef.

SERVES 4

4 x 180g beef tournedos steaks, about
  2.5–4cm thick
100ml good quality red wine
2 sprigs fresh rosemary
8 juniper berries
2 tbsp olive oil
salt and freshly cracked black pepper
1 tbsp brown sugar
2 Granny Smith apples, peeled, cored, cut
  into 1cm thick wedges
1 tbsp cider vinegar
200ml well-flavoured meat stock
1 tbsp redcurrant jelly
2 tbsp fresh redcurrants

FOR THE CHESTNUT BLINIS

175g warm mashed potato
100g unsweetened chestnut purée
75g plain flour
1 egg plus 1 egg yolk
100ml full fat milk
2 tbsp clarified butter (see page 44)

1 Place the beef tournedos in a deep dish, pour the wine over, tuck in the rosemary and sprinkle the juniper berries over. Cover and marinate at room temperature for 1 hour, turning them once or twice. Remove and strain the marinade.

2 Make the blinis. Mix the warm potato, chestnut purée and flour in a bowl, add the eggs, then add enough milk to make a batter that easily drops off a spoon. Season to taste.

3 Heat the clarified butter in a large non-stick frying pan, drop in 2 tbsp batter to make little pancakes about 5mm thick. Make 8 in total. Cook for 2–3 minutes on each side until golden and set, then remove and keep warm.

4 Heat the olive oil in a large non-stick frying pan and, when hot, season the beef and fry until golden all over. Cook the steaks to your particular liking, remove and keep warm.

5 Remove any fat from the pan, add the sugar and apples and caramelise slightly together for 4–5 minutes, remove from the pan.

6 Add the cider vinegar, strained marinade and meat stock to the pan and cook gently until the sauce is reduced by half. Add the redcurrant jelly and stir through; add the redcurrants and then return the apples to the sauce. Season to taste. Serve the beef on the chestnut blinis, coated with the sauce.

Tournedos Rossini

The Italian composer Rossini was a noted gourmand and his love of foie gras and truffles is well known. He certainly had extravagant tastes! This dish was created for him in a Parisian café in his honour. It is expensive to prepare but worth it, as it is a dish that is absolutely memorable.

SERVES 4

3 tbsp clarified butter (see below)
4 x 175g tournedos steaks, all fat removed
salt and freshly cracked black pepper
4 x 90g slices fresh foie gras, 1cm thick
4 x 1cm thick slices baguette bread
150ml Madeira
300ml well-flavoured beef stock (see page 141)
25g unsalted butter, chilled, cut in small pieces
8 slices fresh or preserved truffles, thinly sliced

1 Preheat oven to 200°C. Heat an ovenproof non-stick frying pan until hot, then add 1 tbsp of the clarified butter over a moderate heat. Season the steaks with salt and pepper. Add the steaks to the pan, sear until browned all over and golden brown in colour.

2 Transfer to the oven and cook for 5–6 minutes for medium rare or longer if you prefer. Remove the steaks and keep warm.

3 Return the pan to the heat, add the seasoned foie gras, cook for 30 seconds on high heat. Remove and keep warm.

4 Place another pan on the heat, add the remaining clarified butter and fry each baguette slice until golden, about 30 seconds on each side. Remove and keep warm.

5 Return the foie gras pan a final time to a moderate heat, add the Madeira and stock and bring to the boil rapidly until the liquid is reduced and syrupy, about 15 minutes. Remove from the heat and add the chilled butter to the sauce, a little at a time, until melted.

6 To serve, place a bread crouton on a serving plate, top each with a steak and a slice of foie gras. Arrange the truffle slices on top, pour the sauce over and serve.

TO CLARIFY BUTTER

1 Cut the butter into cubes and place in a pan; heat gently until the milk solids have separated from the fat. Do not let the butter go dark or its fresh taste will be destroyed.

2 Skim off any froth on the surface. Carefully pour the clear liquid butter into a bowl, discarding the milk solids left in the pan. The butter is now ready for use as desired.

Roger's fillet steak mathurini
Fillet steak with armagnac and black pepper–currant sauce

This recipe comes from good friend Roger Verge who last year retired and sold his beautiful restaurant *Moulin de Mougins* in southern France. It is one of the great sauces to serve with pan-fried steak. Roger suggests serving this dish with buttered leaf spinach. The fluffy sweetcorn and potato cakes are also excellent with it.

SERVES 4

40g currants

4 x 175g fillet or tournedos steaks, well trimmed

salt and freshly cracked black pepper

1 tbsp coarsely cracked black peppercorns

50g unsalted butter

30ml vegetable oil

45ml armagnac or cognac

300ml well-flavoured beef stock (see page 141)

buttered leaf spinach, to serve (optional)

FOR THE SWEETCORN–POTATO CAKES

250g mashed potato

200g canned sweetcorn, well drained

75g fresh white breadcrumbs

1 small egg yolk

30ml olive oil

1   Cook the currants in boiling water for 5 minutes, then drain well. Place on one side.

2   Season the steaks liberally with salt and pepper on both sides, then roll them in the cracked peppercorns, pressing them well into the meat with the flat of your hand.

3   Heat half the butter with the oil together in a large frying pan, when foaming add the steaks and cook over a moderate heat until cooked as you like them, turning them from time to time. Remove from the pan and rest (see page 9).

4   Pour off the butter from the pan, add the currants, armagnac away from the heat, then reduce over a low heat. Add the stock, bring to the boil and reduce by two thirds. Whisk in the remaining butter and season to taste.

5   Arrange some buttered cooked spinach on 4 serving plates, top each with a sweetcorn–potato cake, then a cooked steak. Pour the armagnac sauce over and serve.

FOR THE SWEETCORN–POTATO CAKES

1   Place the mashed potato in a bowl and season to taste. Add the sweet corn, breadcrumbs and egg yolk and bind to a firm mix. Shape into 4 evenly sized balls, then flatten to make patties about 1cm thick.

2   Heat the oil in a non-stick frying pan and fry the patties for 2–3 minutes on each side, until golden.

Sechuan peppercorn steak caramelised ginger rice, Asian pickles

This dish is really fresh tasting – and the colours are truly amazing! It is prepared simply and quickly and never disappoints. Try the beef sliced cold on the rice as another alternative.

SERVES 4

4 x 175g sirloin steaks, trimmed of excess fat

3 tbsp light soy sauce

1 tbsp plus 1 tsp brown sugar

2 tsp five-spice powder

1 tbsp Sechuan peppercorns

120ml sunflower oil

2 eggs, lightly beaten

2.5cm piece root ginger, chopped

1 garlic clove, crushed

175g shiitake mushrooms, thickly sliced

500g cooked long grain rice

2 spring onions, shredded

1 tbsp soy sauce

salt and freshly cracked black pepper

FOR THE PICKLE

100ml rice wine vinegar

2 tbsp sugar

1 onion, halved, sliced

1 carrot, shredded

¼ cucumber, deseeded and shredded

1 Place the steaks in a dish, pour the light soy sauce over and add 1 tsp brown sugar. Add the five-spice and peppercorns and marinate the steaks in the mixture for 2 hours, covered, at room temperature.
2 For the pickle, boil the vinegar and sugar for 5 minutes, then pour into a bowl. Add the vegetables, toss well together, and leave to go cold. Drain well.
3 Heat 100ml of the oil in a wok or large frying pan and, when hot, add the beaten egg and stir lightly to scramble it, keeping the egg in large strands. Remove the egg and set on one side.
4 Return the pan to the heat, add the ginger, garlic and 1 tbsp brown sugar and lightly caramelise together for 1 minute.
5 Add the mushrooms, cook for a further minute, then add the cooked rice and stir fry until well amalgamated and lightly caramelised. Add the spring onions, soy sauce and the cooked egg, toss well together and season to taste. Keep warm.
6 Heat a frying pan, add remaining oil and, when hot, remove the steaks from the marinade, season with salt, and add to the pan. Cook until well sealed and golden, about 2–3 minutes on each side. Pour the marinade over and glaze the meat in the marinade. Cook for a further 2 minutes, then remove.
7 Cut each steak into wide strips, arrange on a pile of caramelised rice and pour the pan juices over; garnish with the pickled vegetables and serve.

Basil-crusted beef scaloppine, rocket and Parmesan

The taste of this Italian style steak dish lies in its simplicity.

SERVES 4

8 x 90g small minute steaks, about 5mm thick

2 tbsp prepared pesto sauce

salt and freshly cracked black pepper

2 eggs, beaten

75g fresh white breadcrumbs

4 tbsp sunflower oil

100ml olive oil

2 tbsp balsamic vinegar

1 red onion, halved, thinly sliced

1 garlic clove, crushed

1 red pepper, halved, deseeded, thinly sliced

8 red cherry tomatoes, halved

150g rocket leaves

50g Parmesan cheese, thinly sliced

lemon wedges, to garnish

1 Place the steaks in a dish, pour the pesto sauce over and season with salt and pepper. Pour the eggs over, mix with the steaks and sauce, leave to stand for 1 hour at room temperature. Remove each piece of meat and coat it well in the breadcrumbs.

2 Heat the oil in a large non-stick frying pan and when hot quickly fry the steaks on both sides for 3–4 minutes or until crisp and golden.

3 Meanwhile make the dressing by mixing together the oil and vinegar.

4 Place the onion, garlic, red pepper, tomatoes and rocket in a bowl, add the Parmesan and season to taste. Just before serving add the dressing.

5 Place the pan-fried steaks, 2 per person, on serving plates, place some salad alongside and serve, garnished with lemon wedges.

Filet mignons with anchovy–black olive sauce

Anchovy with beef is not something that immediately springs to mind, but it has been used in Italian and French cooking since time immemorial. It adds depth to the sauce but should not be overdone, or the dish will be spoiled.

SERVES 4

8 x 90g filet mignons, about 1cm thick

1 tbsp olive oil

½ tsp chopped fresh rosemary

½ tsp chopped fresh thyme

salt and freshly cracked black pepper

2 shallots

1 garlic clove, crushed

1 tbsp chopped anchovy fillets

400g canned tomatoes, chopped

¼ tsp lemon zest

2 tbsp red wine vinegar

2 tbsp chopped fresh Italian flat-leaf parsley

12 pitted black olives

1 Place the beef in a bowl, add the olive oil and herbs, cover and marinate for 2 hours at room temperature.

2 Heat a non-stick frying pan on high heat. Remove the filet mignons from the marinade and season with salt and pepper. Add the mignons to the hot pan and cook until golden, about 2 minutes on each side for rare, or to your liking. Remove and keep warm.

3 Add the shallots and garlic to the pan, cook for 1 minute or until softened. Stir in the anchovy and cook for 30 seconds. Add the tomatoes and lemon zest, and cook until the sauce thickens. Add the vinegar and cook for a further minute. Finally add the parsley and olives and season to taste.

4 Spoon the sauce over the beef and serve.

Basil-crusted beef scaloppine,
rocket and Parmesan

Beef piccatas with sage, fontina *con balsamico*

Why is it that balsamic vinegar has made such a great impression on our cooking of recent years? It seems to turn up in everything from sauces, soups, even desserts – I put it down to the British sweet tooth: this vinegar is rich, syrupy and sweet and adds piquancy to dishes while retaining balance.

SERVES 4

8 x 90g filet mignons

4 tbsp olive oil

2 red onions, thinly sliced

2 anchovy fillets, well rinsed, finely chopped

salt and freshly cracked black pepper

100ml balsamic vinegar

100ml well-flavoured beef stock (see page 141)

6 fresh sage leaves, chopped

75g Fontina cheese, thinly sliced

1 Using a kitchen mallet or rolling pin, lightly flatten the beef steaks between some clingfilm.

2 Heat half the olive oil in a large non-stick frying pan. Toss in the onions, and cook for about 10 minutes or until the onions are golden and lightly caramelised. Add the anchovy, mix well and cook for a further 2 minutes. Remove the onion mix and set aside.

3 Heat another large non-stick frying pan and, when hot, add the remaining oil. Season the beef well with salt and pepper, then seal both sides of the beef in the pan for 30 seconds.

4 Pour the balsamic vinegar and stock over, add the sage and reduce down to a thick sauce. Turn the beef in the sauce as it reduces to a syrupy glaze. Add the caramelised onions to the sauce, season and cook for 2 minutes.

5 Place 2 piccata on each serving plate and top with cheese slices. Reheat the onion sauce, then pour it over the beef and serve. I particularly like to serve this dish with some buttery noodles, such as tagliatelle.

Fried steak with black pepper, green chilli and spring onions

Black pepper and chilli team up to add a fantastic peppery hot flavour to the steaks. This dish is an adaptation from a similar dish I tasted in Singapore during my time there.

SERVES 4

800g rump steak, cut into thin strips

2 large garlic cloves, crushed

½ tsp cracked black peppercorns

2.5cm piece root ginger, finely grated

2 tbsp dark soy sauce

100ml sherry

2 tsp brown sugar

2 tbsp sunflower oil

1 tbsp sesame oil

12 small fresh green chillies, halved lengthways, deseeded

6 spring onions, cut into 5cm lengths

1 Place the meat in a bowl, add the garlic, peppercorns, ginger, soy sauce, sherry and sugar, toss well together and leave for 1 hour at room temperature.

2 Heat both the oils in a wok or large frying pan, add the chillies and spring onions and stir fry for 2–3 minutes. Add the meat and its marinade and stir fry for a further 3–4 minutes, toss well and serve.

Beef piccatas with sage,
fontina *con balsamico*

Cashel-stuffed rump steak, celery and herb marmalade

When it comes to a successful partnership, steak and blue cheese is a winning combination. I put it down to the rich complexity of the meat that needs a little piquancy to offset it, and Irish Cashel blue cheese fits that bill. It is mild and creamy – the perfect partner. Another blue cheese such as Stilton or Yorkshire blue would be equally good.

SERVES 4

4 x 200g rump steaks, approx 2.5cm thick
150g Cashel blue cheese
1 tbsp unsalted butter
1 tbsp double cream
2 tbsp chopped walnut pieces
salt and freshly cracked black pepper
2 tbsp sunflower oil
100ml port
150ml well-flavoured beef stock (see page 141)
fresh thyme, to garnish

FOR THE MARMALADE

25g unsalted butter
2 red onions, halved, sliced
½ head celery, peeled, sliced
½ tsp picked fresh thyme leaves
1 tbsp soft brown sugar
250ml red wine
50ml red wine vinegar
1 tbsp redcurrant jelly

1. Using a sharp small knife, cut in a slit in the side of each rump steak to form a deep pocket, taking care not to cut right through the steak.
2. In a bowl, mash the cheese and the butter to a paste, add the cream and walnuts and season lightly.
3. Carefully open up the pockets of the beef and fill each pocket with the cheese mix, ensuring it is well tucked inside the steaks. Close the opening and secure with a cocktail stick. Place the steaks in the fridge for 1 hour to set.
4. For the marmalade, heat the butter in a pan, add the onion and celery and cook for 4–5 minutes until slightly softened. Add the thyme and sugar and lightly caramelise for another 5 minutes over moderate heat. Add the wine and vinegar and simmer gently for 10–12 minutes until all the liquid has evaporated and the vegetables are very soft and sticky in texture. Stir in the redcurrant jelly, season to taste and keep warm.
5. Heat the oil in a non-stick frying pan and, when hot, season the steaks with black pepper and a little salt (as Cashel is quite salty), add to the pan and cook until golden all over, well browned and cooked to your liking. When cooked, remove and keep warm.
6. Remove any excess grease from the pan, add the port and stock and boil to reduce by half until it coats the back of a spoon. Season to taste.
7. Serve the steaks topped with a good heap of the celery marmalade, pour a little port sauce around and serve garnished with fresh thyme. Some buttered spinach or chard would be magnificent with the steaks.

Bistecca alla pizzaiola

One of the great traditional Italian trattoria dishes, one I still enjoy at every opportunity. This sauce, as you would expect, is made with a pizza-type sauce. Try adding a slice of Italian Mozzarella or Provolone on top when finished, then pass it under the grill for 30 seconds – it's good!

SERVES 4

2 tbsp olive oil

4 x 180g sirloin steaks

salt and freshly cracked black pepper

1 onion, thinly sliced

2 garlic cloves, crushed

1 large red pepper, halved, deseeded, thickly sliced

1 large yellow pepper, halved, deseeded, thickly sliced

125g button mushrooms

4 plum tomatoes, peeled, deseeded, chopped

1 tsp tomato purée

1 tbsp chopped fresh oregano

4 tbsp dry white wine

150ml well-flavoured beef stock (see page 141)

4 slices Mozzarella or Provolone (optional)

1 Heat half the olive oil in a large non-stick pan and, when hot, add the seasoned steaks. Cook until golden brown, and to your liking. Remove and keep warm.

2 Add the onion and garlic with remaining oil, cook for 4–5 minutes or until the onion is tender. Add the peppers and mushrooms and cook for further 5 minutes.

3 Add the chopped tomatoes, tomato purée and oregano, and continue to cook for 5 minutes.

4 Pour the white wine into the pan and boil for 2 minutes. Finally, add the stock, simmer for 10 minutes until the sauce is thick and well reduced. Top each steak with a slice of Mozzarella or Provolone and pass it under a hot grill, If you like, then spoon the sauce over and serve.

Beef serundeng

In a modern approach to this Indonesian classic, this is cooked quickly to keep the flavours fresh rather than braised slowly. Galangal is a type of camphorised flavoured ginger available in Thai stores, although root ginger is fine too.

SERVES 4

6 tbsp sunflower oil

2 shallots, finely chopped

2.5cm piece galangal, finely chopped

1 garlic clove, crushed

2 sticks lemongrass, outer casing removed, inner finely chopped

3 tbsp sweet chilli sauce

2 lime leaves

75g unsweetened desiccated coconut

½ tsp ground turmeric

375g sirloin steak, trimmed of all fat, cut into 5mm thick slices

salt and freshly cracked black pepper

1 tsp ground coriander

1 tbsp brown sugar

200ml coconut milk

1 Heat half the oil in a wok or frying pan, add the shallots, galangal, garlic and lemongrass and stir fry until lightly browned. Add the chilli sauce and lime leaves and continue to stir fry for a further 2 minutes. Add the desiccated coconut and turmeric and cook for 1 minute; remove to one side.

2 Heat the remaining oil in another wok or frying pan, lightly season the beef with salt, pepper and ground coriander, and stir fry it in the hot oil for 2–3 minutes or until almost cooked, remove the beef and keep warm.

3 Add the brown sugar to the pan and lightly caramelise it; add the coconut milk, the contents of the first wok and bring to the boil.

4 Return the beef to the sauce and serve with steamed rice.

Julienne of beef Stroganoff

This dish evokes many memories for me. I first prepared it during my early years of training: it is simple to prepare, quick cooking and mildly spicy. It is a dish that you will love to prepare time and time again. Buttered noodles make the ideal accompaniment.

SERVES 4

800g beef fillet tail, cut into finger size strips
salt and freshly cracked black pepper
3 tbsp Hungarian paprika
2 tbsp sunflower oil
1 shallot, finely chopped
8 cocktail gherkins, rinsed, cut into thin shreds
100ml white wine
2 tbsp white wine vinegar
225g button mushrooms, thinly sliced
150ml sour cream or crème fraîche
100ml well-flavoured beef stock (see page 141)
¼ tsp grated lemon zest
¼ tsp Dijon mustard

1 Season the meat with salt, pepper and 2 tbsp of the paprika.

2 Heat a large frying pan with the oil and, when hot, add the meat and fry for 3–4 minutes until golden, then remove and keep warm.

3 Add the shallot and gherkins to the residue in the pan and cook for 1 minute. Pour the wine and wine vinegar over and boil for 2 minutes. Add the mushrooms, sour cream, stock and lemon zest and cook until the sauce is thickened and coats the back of a spoon. Add the mustard and remaining paprika; adjust the seasoning to taste.

4 Return the beef to the sauce and heat through for 1 minute. Serve with hot buttered noodles.

Retro-style steak Diane

The origin of this dish is a little confusing – I've heard as many descriptions of how it came about as I have seen variations in its preparation. So in an effort to please all, here is my recipe the way I've prepared it for many years with great success.

SERVES 4

- 4 x 180g minute sirloin steaks, all fat removed, batted out thinly
- salt and freshly cracked black pepper
- 2 tbsp clarified butter (see page 44)
- 4 banana shallots, peeled, thinly sliced
- 200g button mushrooms, sliced
- 2 tbsp brandy
- 1 tbsp Dijon mustard
- 2 tbsp Worcester sauce
- 200ml well-flavoured meat stock
- juice of ¼ lemon
- 1 tbsp chopped fresh Italian flat-leaf parsley
- ½ tbsp chopped fresh tarragon
- 10g unsalted butter, chilled, cut into small pieces

1. Season the steaks with salt and pepper.
2. Heat the clarified butter in a large non-stick frying pan and, when hot, add 2 steaks at a time and cook over the highest heat for 1 minute each side for medium rare, or longer if you prefer. Reheat the pan and prepare the other 2 steaks the same way. Keep the steaks hot while you make the sauce.
3. Add the shallots and mushrooms to the pan and cook about 4–5 minutes until golden and slightly tender. Add the brandy and cook for 30 seconds. Add the mustard, Worcester sauce, and stock; cook until the sauce is reduced by half and coats the back of a spoon.
4. Finally add the lemon juice, herbs, and stir in the butter; season to taste with salt and pepper. Spoon the sauce over the steaks and serve.

Steak involtini cooked in Parmesan cream

The little rolls known as *involtini* in Italy are filled with a flavourful mixture of cheese, garlic and lemon zest, then finished in a creamy Parmesan sauce.

SERVES 4

8 x 100g filet mignons
20g fresh basil leaves, roughly chopped
½ tsp grated lemon zest
1 garlic clove, crushed
150g Parmigiano Reggiano, cut into
   5 x 5mm thick batons
2 tbsp olive oil
4 tbsp red wine
125ml double cream
20g Parmigiano Reggiano cheese, finely
   grated
salt and freshly cracked black pepper

1. Using a kitchen mallet or rolling pin, lightly bat out the filet mignons between clingfilm.
2. Mix the basil, lemon zest and garlic together in a bowl and spoon over the beef. Top with a baton of cheese then carefully roll each mignon up tightly and secure with a cocktail stick.
3. Heat the oil in a casserole or gratin dish and, when hot, add the beef and seal until golden all over.
4. Pour the red wine over and cook for 2 minutes. Pour the cream over, reduce the heat, cover with a lid, and cook for 6–8 minutes. Remove the mignons from the casserole; remove the cocktail sticks and keep the mignons warm.
5. Whisk the grated cheese into the cream mixture in the casserole and season to taste. Pour over the beef and serve.

Pan roasted rib with green peppercorn-herb crust

CLASSIC ROASTS

Pan roasted rib with green peppercorn–herb crust

This peppercorn-herb crust adds a wonderful texture to the top of the beef, while the inner flavour of the meat remains juicy and tender.

SERVES 2

1 tbsp olive oil
25g unsalted butter
750g rib steak on the bone
salt and freshly cracked black pepper
20g green peppercorns in brine, drained
2 tsp Dijon mustard
2 tbsp chopped fresh mixed herbs
  (e.g. parsley, tarragon, chervil, chives)
1 egg white
30g fresh white breadcrumbs

1 Preheat the oven to 220°C. Heat an ovenproof frying pan on the heat and, when hot, add the oil and butter.

2 Season the rib liberally with salt and pepper all over, place in the pan, and seal it all over until golden. Remove the rib from the pan.

3 In a bowl, crush the peppercorns and mix with the mustard and chopped fresh herbs. Whisk the egg white until very firm, then fold into the peppercorn mixture. Spread a thick layer of the mix onto the rib, then sprinkle the breadcrumbs over.

4 Reheat the frying pan and, when hot, add the beef and baste some of the fat from the pan over the breadcrumbs. Place in the oven and cook for 10–12 minutes for rare or longer if you prefer, ensuring the beef has a crisp crust. Remove and allow the meat to rest before slicing into thick slices.

Rib steak with aged vinegar, shallots and herbs

In this recipe a thick, juicy French-style rib steak is cooked on the bone, for two people, in butter with herbs, then coated in a wonderful vinegar-enriched pan sauce.

SERVES 2

750g rib of beef on the bone
salt and freshly cracked black pepper
1 tsp picked fresh thyme
45ml vegetable oil
50g unsalted butter
4 shallots, finely chopped
125ml good quality, aged red wine vinegar
75ml red wine
150ml well-flavoured beef stock (see
  page 141)
1 tbsp chopped fresh Italian flat-leaf
  parsley
½ tsp Dijon mustard

1 Preheat the oven to 220°C. Season the rib steak liberally all over with salt and pepper, then rub it all over with the thyme and leave for 30 minutes.

2 Heat the oil in a heavy based frying pan suitable for the oven, and when hot, add the beef rib and seal it all over.

3 Add half the butter. Place the pan in the oven and cook for 5–10 minutes on each side, depending on the thickness of the meat and on how you like it cooked. Baste the beef during cooking, ensuring that the butter doesn't burn.

4 Remove the meat from the oven and keep warm (see resting meats page 9).

5 Pour away the excess fat from the pan, add the remaining butter, and the shallots, and cook for 2–3 minutes until softened, but with no colour. Pour the vinegar, wine and stock over and cook for 5 minutes. Add the parsley and mustard and season to taste.

6 Cut the rib into thick slices lengthways and arrange on a serving dish; pour the pan sauce over, and serve, or serve the sauce separately. I suggest serving roasted baby new potatoes and green vegetables, such as purple sprouting broccoli, with the rib.

Rib steak with aged vinegar, shallots and herbs

Prime roast rib of beef with thyme Yorkshire puddings

To enjoy a traditional roast rib of beef at its best, when roasted it must be crisp on the outside while remaining juicy and tender within. Only then will you come to appreciate why we – and overseas visitors to Britain – enjoy it so much. A little port or sherry added to the pan juices after roasting makes a great gravy.

SERVES 8

2kg prepared rib of beef
 (wing rib or fore rib)
salt and freshly cracked
 black pepper
100ml olive oil

FOR THE GRAVY

400ml well-flavoured beef
 stock (see page 141)
1 tbsp redcurrant jelly
2 tbsp cornflour
100ml port or sherry

1 Preheat oven to 220°C. Rub the rib liberally all over with salt and pepper. Heat the oil in a large roasting pan and, when hot, add the beef and seal all over until golden brown. Transfer to the oven and cook for 1 hour 20 minutes for medium rare or to your preferred liking.

2 When cooked, remove the beef from the pan, keep warm and rest it under foil.

3 Pour off any excess oil from pan (reserving it to cook roast potatoes of course!), then pour in the stock and loosen any sticky residue left in the bottom of the pan. Simmer for 5 minutes, then add the redcurrant jelly.

4 Slake the cornflower with the port and thicken the gravy, whisking it into the pan. Season to taste and strain into a sauce boat.

5 Serve the rib with the port gravy and my thyme Yorkshire puddings (see below).

Thyme Yorkshire puddings

250g plain or self raising
 flour
pinch of salt
2 large eggs
250ml full fat milk

1 tsp picked fresh thyme
 leaves
salt and freshly cracked black
 pepper
little oil or dripping

1 In the bowl of an electric mixer, blend the flour with the salt; break in the eggs. Stir them gently together at first then stir until you have a stiff paste. Add a little milk and beat until smooth.

2 Add the remaining milk, 250ml water, the thyme and season well. Leave to stand for 1 hour.

3 Heat little oil in an individual Yorkshire pudding pan, place in the oven and, when smoking, pour in the mix, up to three quarters full. Return to the oven for 20–25 minutes or until the Yorkshires have risen and are crisp. Remove and serve immediately with the roast beef.

Rolled rib of beef with walnut, porcini and raisin stuffing

In this dish all the bones are removed from the rib (ask your butcher to do this), making it easy to carve. Leaving the meat to rest also will give you a better yield and helps make carving easier.

SERVES 8–10

15g dried porcini mushrooms
   soaked in 200ml hot water for
   20 minutes
120g streaky bacon, chopped
75g unsalted butter
1 onion, finely chopped
1 garlic clove, crushed
400g flat-cap mushrooms, chopped
50g raisins
75g walnut pieces, chopped

125g fresh white breadcrumbs
zest of ¼ lemon
3 tbsp chopped fresh Italian flat-leaf
   parsley
salt and freshly cracked black pepper
4kg boneless beef rib (wing or fore)
2 tbsp sunflower oil
125ml Madeira
600ml well-flavoured beef stock (see
   page 141)
2 tbsp cornflour slaked with 2 tbsp Madeira

1 Drain the porcini from their soaking liquid and chop them finely, reserving the liquid.
2 Heat a large frying pan and, when hot, add the bacon and cook until the fat is extracted and the bacon crispy. Add 50g of the butter to the pan, and add the onion, garlic and mushrooms. Cook over a high heat until golden and softened.
3 Add the chopped porcini, raisins, walnuts, breadcrumbs and lemon zest and toss together well. Cook for further 2–3 minutes. Pour the porcini soaking liquid over, add the parsley and season well with salt and pepper. Remove from the heat into a bowl, leave to cool.
4 Preheat the oven to 200°C. Using a sharp knife cut down the length of the beef at the top, down towards the centre. Carefully open up the rib, season it liberally all over.
5 Place the stuffing in the centre of the beef, pressing down well to compact it. Close up the rib at the top and tie the rib around the outside with kitchen string at 5cm intervals to secure it tightly. Season the outside of the beef.
6 Heat the oil in a large roasting pan, add the beef and seal it all over to golden brown, 5–6 minutes. Place in the oven to cook for 1 hour 45 minutes for rare or longer if you prefer. Lift the beef from the pan, place on a dish, cover with foil and keep it warm.
7 Remove excess fat from the pan, leaving any sticky residue in the pan. Add the Madeira and stock and boil for 6–8 minutes. Thicken by whisking in the remaining butter and the cornflour, cook for 1 minute then strain. Carve the beef and serve with the gravy.

Stuffed fillet with Pecorino and rosemary pesto

Stuffing beef always makes an impressive presentation and this dish of Italian origin is a real winner.

SERVES 6
1kg fillet of beef
salt and freshly cracked black
 pepper
100g Pecorino cheese, cut into
 1cm batons
220g thinly sliced Parma ham
2 tbsp sunflower oil

FOR THE PESTO
2 tbsp chopped fresh
 rosemary
20 fresh basil leaves
2 garlic cloves , crushed
6 tbsp olive oil
2 tbsp grated Parmesan

1 Make the pesto; place the herbs, garlic and olive oil in a blender and whiz to a coarse paste. Remove to a bowl, stir in the Parmesan and season lightly. Measure 100ml for use, and refrigerate any excess.

2 Place the fillet on a work surface. Using a sharp knife cut the beef down its length, about 5cm deep, starting and finishing 2.5cm from either end. Open up the beef to form a deep pocket. Season the beef inside the pocket with salt and pepper.

3 Place half the measured pesto in the pocket and spread it out over the length of the fillet. Place the batons of cheese on top of the pesto, then top with remaining pesto and press down lightly. Close up the fillet at the top and carefully roll the fillet in the Parma ham slices, so that it is completely covered.

4 Lightly tie the fillet with kitchen string and place in the fridge to set up for 1 hour.

5 Preheat the oven to 200°C. Heat the oil in the roasting pan on the heat and seal the the fillet all over, then roast for 40 minutes for rare or to your liking. Leave to rest before slicing then serve.

Roast beef with cranberry-beetroot relish, dill yoghurt

A simple elegant cut of beef makes for easy entertaining, it cooks quickly, slices easily, and goes well with numerous sauces or relish. Any other of the sauces for roasts on pages 138–141 will complement the beef, however this sweet and sour relish is one of my particular favourites, served at room temperature on a hot summer day.

SERVES 6

800g piece fillet, well trimmed

2 tbsp sunflower oil

salt and freshly cracked black pepper

FOR THE DILL YOGHURT

100ml natural thick set yoghurt

2 tbsp horseradish relish

½ tsp Dijon mustard

2 tbsp chopped fresh dill

1 Preheat the oven to 240°C. Tie the beef lightly with kitchen string at 2.5cm intervals.
2 Heat the oil in a roasting pan and, when hot, add the well seasoned beef and cook until well sealed and golden brown all over. Transfer to the oven and cook for 16–18 minutes for rare or to your liking. Remove and cool to room temperature.
3 Prepare the Cranberry-Beetroot Relish (see page 142).
4 For the dill yoghurt, mix all the ingredients in a bowl and season to taste.
5 Slice the beef and serve, garnished with the relish, and with the dill yoghurt separately. I recommend some baked new potatoes and mangetout as accompaniments for this dish.

Salt roasted chateaubriand
with fragrant herbs

When the meat is cooked this way it is juicy and tender and not at all salty as you would immediately imagine. Crack the crust at the dinner table for impressive presentation. Use a good quality coarse salt: Maldon sea salt in Britain is considered the best.

SERVES 4

450g plain flour
100g coarse sea salt
1 large egg
175ml iced water
2 x 480g chateaubriand steaks
salt and freshly cracked black pepper
2 tbsp sunflower oil
50g mixed fresh herbs, finely chopped (e.g.
  rosemary, thyme, sage, oregano, parsley)
beaten egg to glaze

1 Preheat oven to 200°C. For the salt crust, mix the flour and salt in a bowl, make a well in the centre, and add the egg and iced water, bring it together to form a dough. Wrap in clingfilm and leave in the fridge for 30 minutes.
2 Season the chateaubriand steaks well with salt and pepper, roll in the oil then into the chopped herbs.
3 Heat a frying pan and, when very hot, add the beef and brown on all sides until golden, about 5 minutes. Allow to cool for 10 minutes.
4 Roll out the salt dough on a floured surface to make 2 x 20cm squares. Place the chateaubriand in the centre of each dough square and wrap tightly around the beef, enclosing it completely. Pinch the edges to seal firmly, then brush all over with the beaten egg glaze. Place seam side up on a baking tray. Roast for 18–20 minutes for rare or longer if you prefer. Remove from the oven and leave for 10 minutes before serving.
5 Crack open the crust, remove the beef, cut into thick slices and serve.

Peppered black beef fillet

This is a interesting preparation I picked up from good friend and Texas chef Dean Fearing. The beef is marinated in herbs, coarse black pepper and molasses, creating a wonderful dark colour and flavour. Dean usually cuts the fillet into steaks before cooking, I have left the fillet whole and roasted it before slicing – either way is great.

SERVES 6

1kg whole centre-cut beef fillet, all fat removed
175ml molasses
2 tbsp balsamic vinegar
2 tbsp fresh coarsely cracked black pepper
2 garlic cloves, crushed
5cm piece root ginger, grated
1 tsp fresh thyme leaves
1 tsp dried chilli flakes
2 tbsp sunflower oil

FOR THE SAUCE

2 tbsp white wine vinegar
250ml well-flavoured beef stock (see page 141)
3 tbsp of the reserved marinade

1 Place the fillet in a large dish. In a bowl combine the molasses, vinegar, pepper and remaining ingredients except the sunflower oil, then pour over the beef. Mix the marinade well with the beef fillet, then cover with clingfilm and refrigerate for 24 hours, turning it occasionally.
2 Preheat oven to 200°C. Remove the meat from the marinade reserving the marinade. Heat a roasting pan with the oil and, when hot, seal the fillet all over until brown, about 3–4 minutes.
3 Place in the oven to roast for 30 minutes for rare or until cooked to your liking. Remove, keep warm and leave the meat to rest.
4 Return the roasting pan to the heat, pour in the vinegar and boil for 2 minutes, scraping up any sediment from the roast. Add the beef stock, the 3 tbsp of marinade and simmer for 8–10 minutes.
5 Slice the beef into thick slices and serve with the pan sauce. I suggest serving this beef with some orange sweet-potato mash, roasted onions and mushrooms: it is delicious!

Roasted skirt steak marchand du vin

Cooked correctly, skirt has the most flavour of any steak to my mind, although it is not considered as exclusive or popular as some other cuts of meat. It does need to be cooked rare to enjoy it to the full.

SERVES 4

1kg skirt steak (flank)
salt and freshly cracked black pepper
2 tbsp olive oil
1 small bunch fresh thyme
20g unsalted butter
4 shallots, finely chopped
450ml good quality red wine
150ml well-flavoured beef stock (see page 141)

1 Preheat oven to 230°C. Season the beef with salt and pepper all over.
2 Heat the olive oil in a roasting pan on the heat and, when very hot, add the beef, and seal it all over until well browned. Cover with half the thyme. Place in the oven and roast for 8–10 minutes for rare, longer if you prefer. Remove the meat from the oven and allow to rest for 10 minutes, keeping it warm.
3 For the sauce, heat half the butter in a pan, add the shallots and the remaining thyme and cook until the shallots are softened, about 2 minutes.
4 Pour the red wine into the pan and boil rapidly to reduce by more than half and the wine becomes syrupy in consistency. Add the stock and boil again to reduce by half. Remove the thyme from the sauce, whisk in the remaining butter.
5 To serve, slice the steak at an angle and pour the shallot sauce over.

Peppered black beef fillet

Beef Wellington

I always use a centre-cut beef fillet for this dish, as it ensures even cooking. The English claim this dish as their own, but the French like to think differently and call it Boeuf en Croûte (beef in pastry). Either way it is a great classic dish that can be served with great aplomb at a dinner party.

SERVES 6

50g unsalted butter

3 shallots, peeled, finely
  chopped

250g flat black mushrooms,
  finely chopped

100ml dry white wine

50g fresh white breadcrumbs

salt and freshly cracked black
  pepper

2 tbsp sunflower oil

1kg centre-cut beef fillet

600g prepared puff pastry
  beaten egg wash

150ml Madeira

100ml well-flavoured beef
  stock (see page 141)

1 tsp arrowroot slaked with
  1 tsp of the Madeira

1 Preheat oven to 190°C. Heat the butter in a frying pan, add the shallots and cook until softened, 2–3 minutes over low heat. Raise the heat, add the mushrooms and cook for a further 5 minutes until tender. Pour the white wine over and boil for 2 minutes, then add the breadcrumbs, salt and pepper. Transfer to a food processor and coarsely process it; remove and allow to cool.

2 Heat the oil in a frying pan, season the meat, and when the oil is hot add the meat and colour it until well browned and crusty all over, including both ends.

3 Roll the pastry into a rectangle, big enough to cover the beef completely. Trim the edges and keep them for decoration. Spread the mushroom mix all over the pastry, leaving a 3cm border around the edge. Brush the border with a little beaten egg wash.

4 Lay the sealed fillet on the pastry and carefully wrap it up tightly like a parcel, pressing the seams together firmly and tucking the ends under. Place the parcel, seam side down on a large baking tray and brush all over liberally with egg wash. Cut the pastry trimmings to decorate the top with a lattice pattern and brush with beaten egg.

5 Place in the oven for 30–35 minutes for medium rare or longer or shorter depending on your preference. Remove to a carving board, leave to rest for 5 minutes before carving.

6 For the sauce, boil the Madeira and stock together until reduced by almost half. Thicken with the slaked arrowroot, season to taste and serve with the beef.

Cajun pan-crusted flank with garlic butter

Although you can buy prepared Cajun spice mixes in delicatessens, I sometimes find them disappointing, I truly find it's better to make up your own blend.

SERVES 4
1.5kg flank steak
2 tsp garlic salt
1 tsp garlic powder
2 tsp cayenne powder
1 tsp paprika
1 tsp ground white pepper
1 tsp cracked black pepper
1 tsp dried thyme
1 tsp dried oregano
2 tbsp olive oil

FOR THE GARLIC BUTTER
50g unsalted butter
2 garlic cloves, crushed
1 tbsp chopped fresh Italian
   flat-leaf parsley
2 tbsp Worcester sauce

1   Cut the flank through its side, without completely cutting right through, and open up the beef. Place the beef between some clingfilm and, using a kitchen mallet or rolling pin, lightly bat out the beef to about 1cm thick. With a small knife, score the top of the beef to allow the Cajun spices to penetrate.

2   Mix all the spices in a bowl and rub into the beef on both sides along with the olive oil; leave to marinate in a dish for 1 hour at room temperature.

3   Preheat the oven to its highest setting. Remove the beef from its dish and roll it up securely with kitchen string at 2.5cm intervals.

4   Heat a dry large frying pan over the heat and, when very hot, add the beef and char it all over until very brown (this will give off a lot of smoke, so use the best possible ventilation or cover with a lid).

5   Place in the oven to roast for about 10–12 minutes or longer if you prefer. When ready, remove and allow to rest for 5 minutes.

6   For the sauce, heat a frying pan until very hot, add the butter and cook until it begins to foam up. Add the garlic and parsley and cook until the mix turns hazelnut in colour and gives off a nutty fragrance. Add the Worcester sauce. To serve, remove the string from the beef, thickly slice it and pour the garlic butter over the beef.

Beef mechoui

A *mechoui* originates in North Africa – it has come to mean whole roast lamb, generally cooked on a spit, slowly rotating over hot coals. The meat – in this case beef rump – is smeared with a spicy paste before being slow-cooked until it is tender enough to be pulled apart with your fingers.

SERVES 6–8

1.3 kilo beef rump, with fat intact
4 tbsp olive oil
175g unsalted butter, softened
3 garlic cloves, crushed
2 tsp paprika
3 tsp ground cumin
1 tsp dried chilli flakes
salt
good pinch of cinnamon
pinch of turmeric

1 Using a small sharp knife, cut small deep slits around the beef at 5cm intervals. Place the beef in baking dish.

2 Make a paste of the remaining ingredients and run it into the slits in the meat, plus all over the surface generally. Cover and leave in a cool place for 6–8 hours, turning it occasionally. Preheat oven to 240°C.

3 Place the beef in the oven for 15 minutes to seal the flavours, add 600ml water, then reduce the heat to 180°C, cook the rump, turning it frequently. Roast for up to 3 hours, the meat should be tender enough to pull apart with your fingers. Transfer to a serving dish, leave to rest for 10 minutes.

4 Serve the beef the classic Moroccan way with warm bread and a cumin salt dip made by mixing 1 tbsp good cumin with 1 tsp salt, and use for dipping the beef pieces in.

Barolo slow-roasted sirloin

Barolo is one of the greatest treasures of the great Italian wines, a truly characteristic full-bodied red that makes a great marinade and sauce for the slow-roasted sirloin. For the best results marinate the loin overnight.

SERVES 6

1.35kg boneless sirloin of beef (leaving on 3mm covering of top fat)
50g pork fat, cut into thin strips
750ml Barolo wine
1 onion, chopped
1 carrot, coarsely chopped
2 garlic cloves, crushed
5 tbsp good quality red wine vinegar
1 tbsp brown sugar
small handful of fresh mixed herbs (e.g. rosemary, thyme, sage, bayleaf)
salt and freshly cracked black pepper
4 tbsp olive oil

1 Using a small sharp knife, make deep incisions all over the beef, then push the pork strips into them. Place the beef in a large dish.

2 Mix all the remaining ingredients except the oil in a bowl, pour over the beef, cover with clingfilm, and leave to marinate overnight in the fridge.

3 Preheat oven to 160°C. Remove the beef from the marinade and dry on kitchen paper. Strain the marinade, reserving the vegetables and herbs, and the strained marinade.

4 Heat the oil in a large roasting pan and, when hot, add the beef and seal it all over until golden. Remove the beef and add the vegetables and herbs to the pan. Fry until the vegetables are golden.

5 Place the beef on top of the vegetables, pour half the marinade over, and place in the oven to cook for 1 hour 45 minutes. Add more marinade to the beef roast as needed to keep the meat moist.

6 Allow the meat to rest for 5–10 minutes, then pour over any pan juices and serve.

Beef mechoui

Braised beef Bourguignon

Braised beef Bourguignon

This is without doubt one of Burgundy's greatest treasures. Marinating the beef overnight allows it to take on the flavour of the aromatic wine and herbs. The ideal accompaniment for this is mashed celeriac or mashed potato.

SERVES 4

1kg blade or rump steak, cut into large
  pieces
1 bottle good quality red wine
3 garlic cloves, crushed
1 fresh bay leaf
2 sprigs fresh thyme
2 tbsp plain flour
salt and freshly cracked black pepper
50g unsalted butter
1 onion, chopped
1 carrot, chopped
200ml well-flavoured beef stock (see
  page 141)
200g streaky bacon or pancetta, cut into
  short strips
200g small shallots
200g small button mushrooms
2 tbsp redcurrant jelly

1 Place the meat, wine, garlic and herbs in a large bowl, cover with clingfilm and leave in the fridge overnight or for at least 4 hours.
2 Preheat the oven to 160°C. Remove the meat from its marinade and dry it in a cloth. Strain the marinade and set it aside. Toss the meat in the flour and season with salt and pepper.
3 Heat half the butter in a large ovenproof casserole. Add the beef and seal it all over until well browned and crusty (you may have to do this in batches). Add the onion and carrot and cook for a further 5 minutes.
4 Pour the reserved marinade over the meat and vegetables, add the stock and bring to the boil, stirring constantly and loosening any residue stuck to the bottom of the casserole. Cover with a lid, place in the oven for 1½ hours.
5 Heat the remaining butter in a frying pan, add the bacon, shallots and mushrooms, and cook until the shallots are slightly softened and the bacon and mushrooms are nicely browned. Add all these to the casserole, return it to the oven and cook for a further 30 minutes.
6 Skim off any excess fat from the surface of the meat, stir in the redcurrant jelly, then adjust the seasoning to taste and serve.

Steak Esterhazy

This braised steak dish is named after Count Esterhazy, a jovial personality who was a regular dinner guest amongst royalty during the time of the Austro-Hungarian empire.

SERVES 4

2 tbsp olive oil
4 x 180g sirloin steaks
salt and freshly cracked black pepper
10g unsalted butter
2 carrots, cut into 5mm dice
2 sticks celery, cut into 5mm dice
1 onion, chopped
1 tbsp Hungarian paprika
1 tbsp plain flour
600ml well-flavoured beef stock (see
  page 141)
100ml tomato passata
2 tbsp superfine capers, rinsed, drained
1 tbsp Worcester sauce
4 tbsp sour cream
juice of ½ lemon

1 Preheat the oven to 200°C. Heat the oil in an ovenproof casserole; season the steaks liberally all over with salt and pepper. When the oil is hot, add the steaks and seal until golden all over. Remove the steaks to one side.
2 Return the casserole to the heat and add the butter. Toss in the carrots, celery and onion along with the paprika, and cook for 3–4 minutes. Stir in the flour and cook for 2 minutes.
3 Add the stock and passata, stir to the boil. Add the capers and Worcester sauce, then return the beef to the sauce. Cover the casserole with a lid, place in the oven and cook for 25–30 minutes or until the meat and vegetables are tender. Remove the steaks from the sauce.
4 Add the sour cream to the sauce, adjust the seasoning, and finally stir in the lemon juice. Return the steaks to the sauce and serve.

Steak Esterhazy

Braised steak in Irish ale and herbed horseradish dumplings

These topside steaks require slow braising to cook them to melting tenderness. This is one of my favourite ways to enjoy braised steak – the ideal meal for a cold winter's day. Real ale is now a very fashionable drink, and this dish uses Irish ale, a rare treat. Some small boiled carrots tossed in butter would be wonderful with the braised steak.

SERVES 4

1kg stewing feather steaks, trimmed
  of excess fat
2 tbsp plain flour
4 tbsp sunflower oil
2 onions, finely sliced
2 tsp brown sugar
½ tsp mustard powder
1 tbsp tomato purée
1 tsp fresh thyme leaves
1 fresh bay leaf
600ml Irish ale
salt and freshly cracked black pepper
chopped fresh Italian flat-leaf parsley,
  to serve

1 Preheat the oven to 160°C. Coat the topside steaks liberally with the flour.
2 Heat the oil in an ovenproof casserole and fry the steaks in batches until golden all over, remove from the pan and set aside.
3 Add the sliced onions, and fry until well browned. Add the sugar, mustard powder, tomato purée, thyme, bay leaf and ale, and bring to the boil. Season lightly, then return the steaks to the sauce. Cover the casserole and cook in the oven for 2–2¼ hours.
4 Meanwhile make the dumplings. Mix the breadcrumbs, flour, suet, baking powder and chopped thyme together, and season to taste. Bind with the eggs to form a dough.
5 Divide the dough into 12 evenly size balls, coating in a little flour so they do not stick. Poke a hole in each ball, then fill with a little horseradish sauce. Close the hole and re-roll gently to seal well; leave on one side.
6 About 25 minutes before the braised topside is ready, cook the dumplings in a large pan of gently simmering water.
7 To serve, spoon the steaks onto hot plates, coat with the sauce and top with the dumplings. Sprinkle the chopped parsley over before serving.

FOR THE DUMPLINGS
100g fresh white breadcrumbs
100g plain flour
100g shredded suet
1 tsp baking powder
1 tsp finely chopped fresh thyme leaves
2 eggs, beaten
horseradish sauce (see page 141, or bought)

Braised steak Provençale or Daube Provençale

The cut for this dish is feather steak or rump steak rather than the chuck steak used in Provence. The steaks are first marinated then slow-braised in rich orange-flavoured red wine and rosemary sauce. In France it is cooked in a sealed pot called a *daubière*, but any ovenproof casserole is just fine. Baked pasta gratin goes well with this beef dish.

SERVES 4

4 x 200g feather or rump steaks, 2cm thick
700ml good quality red wine
2 carrots, peeled, cut into large chunks
1 onion, peeled, quartered
2 tbsp olive oil
1 tsp chopped fresh rosemary
2 garlic cloves, halved
2 fresh bay leaves
zest and juice of 1 large orange
50g plain flour
75g pancetta or bacon, finely chopped
1 tsp tomato purée
salt and freshly cracked black pepper

1 Place the beef in a dish, pour the wine over, and add the vegetables, olive oil, rosemary, garlic and bay leaves, along with the zest and juice of the orange. Cover and marinate overnight in the fridge.

2 Preheat oven to 180°C. Remove the beef and vegetables from their marinade, pat them dry with a cloth, and reserve the marinade liquid and herbs. Coat the beef with the flour.

3 Heat an ovenproof casserole and add the pancetta and cook for 5 minutes. Add the beef and seal all over until golden, remove the beef and set aside.

4 Add the vegetables and fry until golden. Add the tomato purée and cook for 1 minute. Pour in the marinade and bring to the boil.

5 Return the beef to the sauce, cover the casserole, and cook in the oven for 1½–2 hours or until the beef is tender.

6 Remove the beef and keep it warm, then strain the sauce through a fine strainer. Reduce the sauce until it coats the back of a spoon and season to taste with salt and pepper. Serve the beef with the sauce poured over.

1. Preheat oven to 200°C. Toss the steak well in the flour. Heat the oil in a large ovenproof casserole and, when hot, add the beef and cook until golden brown all over. Remove the beef from the pan.

2. Add the butter to the pan and return to the heat. Add the onions and mushrooms and fry for 3–4 minutes until tender.

3. Return the beef to the pan, add the tomato purée and mix well. Cook for 2–3 minutes. Pour the Worcester sauce and stock over and bring to the boil.

4. Bring a pan of water to the boil, add the kidneys and cook for 2 minutes. Drain them and refresh under cold water; dry in a cloth.

5. Add the kidneys to the beef, cover with a lid, cook in the oven for 1–1¼ hours or until the meat is tender.

6. Roll out the pastry on a floured surface. Place a pie funnel into the centre of a large pie dish. Spoon the steak and kidney mixture around the funnel. Brush the edge of the pie dish with water.

7. Carefully place the pastry over the meat, piercing the pastry to allow the top of the pie funnel to come through. Trim round the edge of the pie dish with a knife. Brush the surface of the pastry with the egg wash.

8. Bake in the oven until the pastry is golden and crusty, about 20–25 minutes. Serve with vegetables of your choice.

VARIATION: STEAK AND OYSTER PIE

One of the great old ways to prepare steak pie during the eighteenth century was to replace the kidneys with oysters. Follow the recipe above, omitting the kidneys. When filling the pie dish, stir some freshly shucked oysters into the beef mix, then cover with the pastry and continue as above.

Steak and kidney pie

This is of the great British dishes – and one of which we can be proud! Ask your butcher for veal kidneys, they are a little more expensive than other kidneys, but the taste of the pie will be very much better. Rump steak or chuck steak are great here.

SERVES 6

850g rump steak or chuck steak

2 tbsp plain flour

4 tbsp sunflower oil

25g unsalted butter

2 onions, finely chopped

200g button mushrooms

1 tbsp tomato purée

2 tbsp Worcester sauce

900ml well-flavoured beef stock (see page 141)

500g veal kidneys, trimmed of membranes and fat, cut into nugget size pieces

400g ready-made puff pastry

beaten egg wash

Cottage pie with a difference

Cottage pie is one of the best loved dishes in the British repertoire, a warming comfort food to defy our cold winter weather. In a break with tradition I have flavoured the mashed potato topping with leeks and wholegrain mustard, and have added a dash of red wine to the meat filling – why not?

SERVES 4

100ml olive oil

2 onions, finely chopped

2 carrots, finely diced

2 parsnips, finely diced

1 garlic clove, crushed

1 tsp dried oregano

700g rump steak, very finely diced

salt and freshly cracked black pepper

400g canned chopped tomatoes

200ml well-flavoured beef stock (see page 141)

100ml red wine

2 tbsp tomato ketchup

2 tsp chopped fresh Italian flat-leaf parsley

½ tsp ground allspice

dash of Worcester sauce

FOR THE TOPPING

650g floury potatoes, peeled

125ml full fat milk

25g unsalted butter, plus a little for topping the potatoes

1 leek, finely chopped

2 tbsp wholegrain mustard

2 egg yolks

1 Preheat oven to 200°C. Heat half the olive oil in a large pan, add the onions, carrots, parsnips, garlic and oregano, and cook over moderate heat until the vegetables are softened, about 10 minutes. Remove them to a bowl.

2 Return the pan to the heat, add the remaining oil and, when hot, season the steak and fry until golden brown, about 6–8 minutes.

3 Add the tomatoes, stock, wine, ketchup, parsley, allspice and Worcester sauce and cook for 5 minutes. Return the vegetables to the pan and simmer for 15 minutes.

4 Make the topping. Cook the potatoes in boiling salted water until tender. Drain well and mash with the milk. Heat the butter in a small pan, add the chopped leek and cook until soft, about 3–4 minutes, then add to the mash. Add the mustard and beat in the egg yolks and season to taste.

5 Place the filling in an ovenproof dish, top with the leek and potato mash and dot with a little butter over the surface. Bake in the oven for 15–20 minutes or until the top is golden brown. Serve with green vegetables of your choice.

Cornish pasties

The pasties' popularity in the West Country was originally due to the development of tin mining in the county of Cornwall. The pasties – filled with beef, usually skirt meat, potatoes and other vegetables – were created for the men as a nutritious meal to eat down the mines. Originally, it would have had savoury beef at one end of the pasty and a sweet offering of apple, jam or treacle at the other: a main course and dessert all in one! Nowadays, the pasty enjoys its good reputation using best quality beef, and its popularity is as strong as ever. For the best results for the pastry, the lard and butter must be used from the freezer.

SERVES 4

FOR THE FILLING
450g skirt or rump steak
700g new potatoes, peeled
400g swede, peeled
1 large onion, finely chopped
salt and freshly cracked black pepper
little beaten egg glaze

FOR THE PASTRY
450g strong plain flour
100g hard butter
100g lard
about 175ml water

1 First make the pastry; sift the flour into a bowl with a good pinch of salt. Cut both the butter and lard into small pieces, then rub into the flour until the mixture is fine and falls through your fingers. Remove to a lightly floured table and make a well in the centre. Add water, a little at a time, until it forms a pliable but stiff dough.

2 Chop the steak finely and place in a bowl. Dice the potatoes and swede, and add to the bowl with the onion. Season well with salt and black pepper and mix well.

3 Divide the pastry into 4 and roll out a piece to a circle about the size of a side plate. Place a pile of the filling in the centre of the dough. Brush the edges of the dough with water or little milk, then bring up the dough together at the top and press together. Working from one end of the pasty to the other, create a rope like design to seal the pastry. Repeat to make 3 more pasties. Chill for 1 hour.

4 Preheat oven to 180°C. Make a small slit at the top of each pasty to let the steam out. Brush with a little beaten egg and place on a lightly greased baking tray, leaving a gap in between them.

5 Bake for 50 minutes or until the pasties are cooked and their undersides have turned brown and crisp. In the traditional manner, serve with a good beer or Cornish-style ale.

Swedish-style beef olives (oxrullader)

The northern Europeans, especially the Scandinavian countries, have a great love for slow braised beef dishes, usually thinly sliced beef rolled with all manner of tasty ingredients. These Swedish 'olives', as they are known, are delicious – great served with noodles or creamy mashed potatoes and cabbage.

SERVES 4

600g beef fillet, cut into 8 thin slices
salt and freshly cracked black pepper
4 tbsp Dijon or Swedish mustard
8 slices streaky bacon
1 onion, finely chopped
2 sweet pickled cucumbers, cut into strips
50g unsalted butter
**600ml well-flavoured beef stock (see
  page 141)**
1 tbsp soy sauce
175ml whipping cream
2 tbsp cornflour
noodles to serve (optional)
chopped fresh Italian flat-leaf parsley

1 Using a kitchen mallet or rolling pin, lightly bat out the beef between some clingfilm. Lay out the slices on a work surface. Season the beef liberally with salt and pepper. Spread the mustard over the beef.
2 Lay 2 slices of streaky bacon on top of each beef slice, then sprinkle over the onion and top with the pickled cucumber strips.
3 Roll up each slice of beef carefully so that the filling remains firmly inside. Secure with a cocktail stick along the join of the roll.
4 Heat the butter in a large frying pan and, when hot, add the rolls and seal until golden all over. Pour the stock and soy sauce over and bring to the boil. Cover and simmer for 30–35 minutes (alternatively, place in the oven at 180°C).
5 When cooked, lift out the beef rolls from the sauce and keep them warm.
6 Mix the cream with the cornflour, add to the stock and simmer for 5–6 minutes until the sauce is thickened to coat the back of a spoon. Season to taste. Serve the beef rolls on a bed of noodles, if you like, and scatter with the parsley. Serve the sauce separately.

Poached salt beef with vegetables, horseradish sauce

In this recipe, I replace the usual cuts associated with salting, such as topside or brisket, with tender chateaubriand. It is lightly salted overnight, then poached with vegetables in an aromatic broth.

SERVES 2

1 x 450–550g chateaubriand steak

30g coarse salt; cracked black pepper

4 sprigs of fresh thyme

1 small bay leaf

1 litre well-flavoured beef stock (see page 141)

2 carrots, peeled, halved lengthways

1 turnip, peeled, cut into wedges

2 sticks celery, cut into 5cm lengths

1 leek, cut into 2.5cm lengths

15g unsalted butter

1 tsp chopped fresh Italian flat-leaf parsley

1 Place the chateaubriand in a bowl, add the salt, half the thyme, the bay leaf and pepper; lightly massage it into the beef and leave covered in the fridge for 12 hours.

2 Rinse off the cure under a little running water, then dry the steak in a cloth.

3 Bring the stock to the boil with the remaining thyme; reduce the heat and cook the vegetables in the stock, retaining a little bite, remove them and keep warm.

4 Return the stock to the heat, add the beef and lightly poach it for 15 minutes.

5 Strain off 100ml of the poaching stock and whisk in the butter to enrich it. Add the parsley and season to taste. (The remaining stock can be frozen for later use.)

6 Slice the beef into 6 slices, garnish with the vegetables, pour the parsley sauce over and serve with the horseradish sauce on the side.

TO SERVE

150ml horseradish sauce (see page 141)

Farsu magru (rolled, braised steak Sicilian style)

Farsu magru literally translates as 'false lean' – a strange name for these little Italian beefsteak rolls stuffed with cheese and herbs, in a rich tomato and red-wine sauce. I like to serve them with a creamy blue-cheese polenta using Gorgonzola cheese. In other parts of Italy this dish is called *braciole*.

SERVES 4

1.5kg beef topside, thinly sliced into
  5mm thick steaks
350g ground beef
75g fresh white breadcrumbs
100g Provolone cheese, grated
75g mortadella sausage, diced
40g raisins, soaked for 20 minutes in hot
  water, drained
2 eggs, hard boiled, finely chopped
1 garlic clove, crushed
40g fresh Italian flat-leaf parsley, chopped
olive oil for cooking
salt and freshly cracked black pepper
1 onion, finely chopped
1 tbsp chopped fresh oregano
800g canned tomatoes, chopped
1 tbsp tomato purée
200ml red wine

1 Using a kitchen mallet or steak bat, lightly flatten the topside steaks.
2 In a bowl, combine the ground beef, breadcrumbs, cheese, sausage, raisins and eggs. Add the garlic and parsley, and mix well together.
3 Spread an even layer of the stuffing over each batted-out steak, folding in the sides and rolling each into a small parcel. Secure each with a cocktail stick or thin kitchen string.
4 Heat a heatproof casserole on the stove with a little oil, season the parcels and fry them until golden all over. When all are sealed, transfer to a plate.
5 To the same pan, add the onion and oregano, and cook until softened, about 3–4 minutes. Add the tomatoes, tomato purée, and red wine, along with 200ml of water.
6 Return the parcels to the casserole, reduce the heat, cover the pan with a lid and simmer for up to 2 hours, adding a little more wine or water if necessary, and ensuring the meat is always covered.
7 Remove the cocktail sticks before serving the rolls on a bed of creamy cheese polenta, coated with the rich wine sauce.

Thai beef salad

Thai beef salad

In Thailand this salad dish is known as *larb neua*: it is wonderfully light, tasty and – for me – evokes many great memories of my time in that beautiful country.

SERVES 4
juice of 1 lime
400g rib-eye or sirloin steak, cut into
   small dice or coarsely chopped
1 iceberg lettuce, outer leaves removed
75g French beans, cooked
1 carrot, shredded
4 spring onions, shredded
2 banana shallots, thinly sliced
25g fresh coriander leaves
25g fresh mint leaves
2 tbsp roasted basmati rice (see right)

FOR THE DRESSING
1 green chilli
1 tbsp palm or brown sugar
juice of 4 limes, zest of 1 lime
4 tbsp fish sauce (*nam pla*)

1 Make the dressing. Crush the green chilli, sugar and lime zest to a paste in a mortar. Add the fish sauce and lime juice.
2 Bring 4 tbsp of water to the boil with the lime juice. Add the diced beef, stirring to break up the meat, and cook for 3–4 minutes or until the beef is cooked. Remove to a bowl and allow to cool.
3 Remove 4 nice cup-shaped lettuce leaves and reserve. Shred the remainder finely. Toss the shredded lettuce with the prepared dressing and remaining vegetables and herbs, adding more fish sauce and lime juice if necessary.
4 Arrange the salad and diced beef in the 4 lettuce cups. Scatter the roasted rice over and serve immediately.

FOR THE ROASTED RICE
1 To prepare the Asian-style rice, heat the oven to 180°C, place basmati rice on a baking tray and dry roast in the oven for 25 minutes until golden. Remove and allow to cool.
2 Crush in a mortar to a coarse powder. Keep sealed in a jar, ready for use.

Bistro steak salad

This salad has all the hallmarks of simple French eating – good steak, creamy Roquefort cheese and crisp bread. I was at a loss as to what to call it until a French chef friend said why not 'bistro salad', and it seemed the perfect description.

650g flank steak (onglet)
salt and freshly cracked black pepper
3 tbsp olive oil
1 tbsp walnut oil
1 tbsp red wine vinegar
1 tsp Dijon mustard
75g Roquefort cheese, crumbled
2 plum tomatoes, cut into large chunks
2 sticks celery, peeled, thinly sliced
1 tbsp walnuts, broken into small pieces
4 handfuls mixed salad leaves
1 small French baguette

1 Heat a chargrill or pan grill until smoking. Season the flank steak with salt and pepper and rub 1 tablespoon of the olive oil over the meat. Cook the flank steak until charred all over, about 5–6 minutes for rare or longer if preferred; remove the meat and allow to rest.
2 Meanwhile make a dressing of the remaining olive oil, walnut oil, vinegar and mustard.
3 Take 25g of the Roquefort, the tomatoes, celery and walnuts in a bowl, pour the dressing over and toss well. Finally, add the salad leaves and toss the whole together.
4 Cut the baguette into thin slices and place on the grill to toast, then toss through the salad. Divide the salad between 4 plates and crumble a quarter of the remaining Roquefort over each salad portion.
5 Slice the flank into thin slices, and place on top of the salad. Serve immediately.

Bistro steak salad

Caramelised beef salad with
mango and sweet anise dressing

Caramelised beef salad with mango and sweet anise dressing

The flavours of this salad are fresh and punchy, depending on your chilli tolerance levels. Be sure to cook the beef very quickly and in a hot pan to ensure a delicate caramelisation and flavour. *Ketjap manis* is available from good Oriental stores.

SERVES 4

500g flank steak or fillet steak, trimmed of all visible fat, thinly sliced
125ml *ketjap manis* (Indonesian soy sauce)
45ml vegetable oil
2 garlic cloves, crushed
½ tsp ground cinnamon
1 tsp ground star anis
2 tbsp brown sugar
1 tbsp fish sauce (*nam pla*)
50g cashew nuts, toasted, coarsely chopped
1 green mango, peeled and finely shredded
4 spring onions, shredded
50g chopped fresh Thai basil
50g chopped fresh mint leaves

FOR THE DRESSING

20g brown sugar
65ml soy sauce
2 tbsp sweet chilli sauce
2 tbsp lime juice
2 tsp fish sauce (*nam pla*)
½ tsp ground star anise

1 Place the thinly sliced steak in a bowl, pour the *ketjap manis* over, mix well, and leave for 30 minutes.
2 Mix all the ingredients for the dressing together in a bowl.
3 Heat the oil in a wok or large frying pan. Stir in the garlic and spices and cook for 1 minute.
4 Over a high heat, add the beef and quickly wok fry for 2 minutes. Sprinkle the sugar and *nam pla* over, and glaze the meat in the sticky sauce.
5 Transfer the beef to a bowl, pour the dressing over, add the remaining ingredients, and toss together. Divide among 4 serving plates or bowls and serve warm.

Beef-macaroni salad with truffle oil, blue cheese dressing

A great way to use up cooked steak, the pasta and blue cheese dressing add bulk to the dish, making it a great main course salad dish. Goat's cheese makes a good alternative to the blue cheese.

SERVES 4

300g macaroni pasta
juice of 1 lemon
4 tbsp olive oil
salt and freshly cracked black pepper
1 red onion, halved, thinly sliced
1 carrot, cut into fine strips
175g snow peas, blanched
300g cold cooked steak, any variety, thinly sliced
150g mixed salad leaves
75g mild blue cheese
4 tbsp good quality mayonnaise
4 tbsp sour cream
1 tbsp truffle oil

1 Cook the macaroni in boiling salted water until *al dente*, following the packet instructions; drain well in a colander.
2 Place in a bowl, add the lemon juice, olive oil and season well.
3 Add the vegetables, thinly sliced beef and the salad leaves; toss it all together.
4 Place the cheese in a bowl, stir in 3 tablespoons of hot water and mix until smooth. Stir in the mayonnaise, sour cream and season lightly.
5 Arrange the salad, piled high in shallow salad bowls, and drizzle the blue cheese–cream dressing over and finally drizzle the truffle oil over. Serve at room temperature.

Beef tataki with lemon soy and pickled vegetables

The term *tataki* in Japan refers to a cut of meat or fish that is lightly seared then rare cooked, chilled, marinated and thinly sliced. Traditional accompaniments are grated, mouli (white radish) with ginger, but I serve mine with a small relish of various ingredients including sweet pickled cucumbers and green onions and soy. Either fillet or sirloin make the best *tataki*.

SERVES 4

750g well trimmed fillet or sirloin steak
salt and freshly cracked black pepper
8 tbsp soy sauce
2 tbsp sunflower oil
1 garlic clove, crushed
4 tbsp mirin (Japanese rice wine)
2 tbsp brown sugar
juice of 2 lemons
2 large sweet dill pickled cucumbers,
  thinly shredded
4 spring onions, thickly shredded
2 tbsp pickled pink ginger slices
150g mouli radish, peeled, finely shredded
15g shiso leaves (optional)
lemon wedges to garnish

1 Preheat the oven to 200°C. Season the beef with salt and pepper then rub 2 tablespoons of the soy sauce onto the beef. Heat an ovenproof frying pan over a high heat, add the sunflower oil and, when smoking, add the beef and seal it all over until brown, turning it often.

2 Transfer to the oven, roast for 12–15 minutes. Ideally use a thermometer, inserted into the centre of the meat, to check the temperature is 55°C, remove and allow the meat to cool.

3 Meanwhile, combine the remaining soy sauce, garlic, mirin, sugar and lemon juice and pour into a deep dish. Place the beef in the marinade, cover and refrigerate for 24 hours, turning it occasionally in the marinade.

4 Remove the beef from the marinade and allow to stand for 30 minutes at room temperature. Slice the beef and arrange the slices, overlapping, on 4 serving plates.

5 In a bowl, toss the cucumbers, spring onions, ginger and mouli radish and add 2–3 tablespoons of the marinade, toss together.

6 Garnish the beef with a pile of the cucumber mixture, sprinkle over the shiso leaves, if using, garnish with the lemon wedges and serve.

Seared beef carpaccio with fennel, anchovy, black olive crème fraîche

This pan-seared beef carpaccio is a variation of the classic raw beef one invented at the famous Harry's Bar in Venice. The crisp fennel adds just the right texture to the dish, while the sour cream adds a pleasant sourness that complements it beautifully.

450g thin beef fillet, well trimmed and
 free of all fat and sinew
salt and freshly cracked black pepper
75ml extra virgin olive oil
2 heads fennel
150g cooked new potatoes, peeled, thickly
 sliced
2 shallots, thinly sliced
juice of ½ lemon
½ garlic clove, crushed
2 anchovy fillets, rinsed, chopped
10ml balsamic vinegar
125g rocket leaves
50g thinly shaved Parmigiano Reggiano
 cheese

FOR THE OLIVE CRÈME FRAÎCHE
125ml crème fraîche
40g good quality black olives, pitted and
 finely chopped

1 Heat a heavy based frying pan over a high heat until very hot. Season the beef well and brush all over with 30ml of the oil. Seal the beef in the very hot pan for 1 minute on each side, until charred on the outside, but very rare in the middle; remove and allow to go cold.

2 Slice the fennel very thinly on a kitchen mandolin or with a sharp knife, place in a bowl, reserving the fennel fronds. Add the potatoes and shallots.

3 Whisk together the lemon juice, garlic, anchovy and vinegar with the remaining olive oil to form a light dressing. Roughly chop the reserved fennel fronds and add them to the dressing, mix well. Season to taste. Drizzle the dressing over the fennel and potatoes and toss to coat evenly. Mix the crème fraîche with the chopped olives.

4 To serve, slice the beef into 5mm slices, divide between 4 serving plates and season lightly with salt and pepper. Add the rocket to the fennel and potatoes, toss together, then arrange the salad on the beef. Scatter the shaved Parmesan over, then garnish with a good dollop of olive crème fraîche to one side; serve at once.

Carpaccio-wrapped buffalo Mozzarella with tuna sauce

Thinly sliced beef, prepared in carpaccio style, is normally served with thinly shaved Parmesan, but Mozzarella works equally well. The tuna mayonnaise that accompanies it makes for an interesting dish.

SERVES 4
400g piece beef fillet, very well chilled
1 buffalo Mozzarella, cut into 8 slices
salt and freshly cracked black pepper
50g canned tuna in oil, well drained
4 tbsp good quality mayonnaise
1 tbsp superfine capers, rinsed, drained
1 garlic clove, crushed
1 tbsp fresh lemon juice
4 tbsp olive oil
1 tbsp balsamic vinegar
2 tomatoes, cut into small dice
1 tbsp chopped black olives
50g rocket leaves
lemon wedges, to garnish

1 Using a long very sharp knife, slice the chilled beef into 8 thin slices. Lay them on a work surface, then top each with a slice of Mozzarella, season with salt and a good amount of pepper and wrap up to enclose the cheese in the beef. Season liberally with salt and pepper all over the exterior.

2 In a blender, whiz together the tuna, mayonnaise, capers, garlic and lemon juice to a smooth purée and season to taste.

3 In a bowl whisk together the oil and vinegar, then add the tomatoes and olives and season lightly.

4 To serve, spoon some tuna sauce into the centre of 4 plates, top with two beef parcels. Dress the top of the beef with a little rocket, then drizzle the tomato and olive dressing over. Garnish with the lemon wedges and serve.

Seared beef carpaccio with fennel, anchovy, black olive crème fraîche

Bresaola

One way to enjoy cold beef, this recipe of *bresaola* is a traditional Italian dish I really enjoyed when I teamed up with chef friend Franco Taruschio when we appeared on the 'Take Six Chefs' TV show, over twenty years ago. Franco and Ann, his wife, have since retired from their famous Walnut Tree Inn in Wales. This recipe is taken from Franco's superb book *Leaves from the Walnut Tree* and is great for a large gathering. Do not attempt to preserve a smaller piece of beef; it is not satisfactory. *Bresaola*, like Parma ham, has a long life and keeps well for three months.

SERVES 25
4kg beef topside
extra virgin olive oil
freshly cracked black pepper
chopped fresh chives
lemon wedges, to garnish

1 Trim the joint of beef, removing all fat and sinews.
2 Put all the ingredients for the marinade in a large bowl, add the meat, cover and leave for one week in a cool place, or until the meat feels firm.
3 Hang the meat in a dry airy place for another week until it feels firm enough to be sliced thinly, it will feel solid, with no give at all as you press with your fingers.
4 Rub the joint with olive oil, wrap in greaseproof paper, and keep in the fridge until required.
5 To serve, slice very thinly, drizzle with olive oil, and season with pepper and chives. Garnish with lemon wedges and serve.

FOR THE MARINADE
equal amounts of red and white wine,
  enough to cover the beef
750g coarse sea salt
12 dried red chillies
24 cloves
12 fresh bay leaves
large bunch of fresh rosemary
3 garlic cloves, crushed
40 black peppercorns
4 strips of orange peel

My steak tartare with crispy potatoes, truffle crème fraîche

Steak tartare has been popular ever since the days of the trendy Parisian bistros. Although I love the classic preparation, I've created one that I think just goes one better.

SERVES 4

sunflower oil for deep frying

250g waxy potatoes, peeled, thinly sliced

400g beef fillet, sirloin or rump, very well chilled

4 cocktail gherkins, rinsed, chopped

2 shallots, finely chopped

2 free range eggs

2 anchovy fillets, rinsed, finely chopped

1 tbsp superfine capers, rinsed, chopped

1 tbsp chopped fresh Italian flat-leaf parsley

1 tsp Dijon mustard

salt and freshly cracked black pepper

50g mâche (lamb's lettuce) salad, to garnish

1   Fill a deep fryer or large saucepan with oil and heat to 180°C. Dry the potatoes well and fry them in batches if necessary until golden and crisp. Drain on kitchen paper and keep warm.

2   For the truffle crème fraîche, mix the mayonnaise with the truffle oil and crème fraîche in a bowl, chill until needed.

3   Trim the beef carefully of any fat or tissue, place on a chopping board and slice into strips. Cut the strips crosswise into very small dice, then chop them briefly with a large knife.

4   Place the steak in a bowl, add the remaining ingredients except the salad, and season with salt and pepper. Gently mix together with a fork. Using wet clean hands, or a metal ring, mould the meat into 4 individual patties and place on 4 serving plates.

5   Place a good dollop of the crème fraîche in the centre of each patty, then garnish the crème fraîche with some chive batons. Garnish the steak tartare with a bouquet of mâche salad and a small pile of the warm potato crisps. Serve immediately.

FOR THE TRUFFLE CRÈME FRAÎCHE

2 tbsp good quality mayonnaise

2 tsp truffle oil

4 tbsp crème fraîche

1 tbsp fresh chives, cut in 2.5cm lengths

Asian-style steak tartare

Serving steak raw allows you to experiment with a whole host of different flavours to complement and enhance it. This oriental inspired tartare is also great spread on small canapé bases to serve with drinks.

SERVES 4

400g beef fillet or sirloin, very well chilled
1 stick lemongrass, outer casing removed, inner finely chopped
2 shallots, finely chopped
2 tbsp *ketjap manis* (Indonesian soy sauce)
2 tbsp chopped fresh coriander
1 tbsp mango chutney, finely chopped
½ tsp wasabi (Japanese horseradish)
½ tsp chopped pickled ginger
salt and freshly cracked black pepper
4 quail eggs
lemon wedges, to garnish
shiso leaves, to garnish

1 Trim the beef carefully of any fat or tissue, place on a chopping board and slice into strips. Cut the strips crosswise into very small dice, then chop it with a large knife briefly.
2 Place in a bowl and add all the remaining ingredients except the quails eggs.
3 Using wet hands, or a metal ring, mould a quarter of the steak tartare onto each of 4 individual plates; remove the metal ring if used.
4 Using your fingers, make a small indentation in the centre of each steak tartare. Fill each hollow with a raw quails' egg. Garnish with the lemon wedges and shiso, then serve.

Beef polpetti with pesto, sundried tomato–*bocconcini* salsa

This dish makes a great light lunch. If you can make your own pesto, so much the better, but there are some good quality ones now on the market.

SERVES 4

1 small French baguette
5 tbsp olive oil
3 tbsp prepared pesto
1 tbsp fresh lemon juice
salt and freshly cracked black pepper
425g minced rib steak or flank
1 small onion, finely chopped
1 garlic clove, crushed
pre-soaked wooden skewers

FOR THE SALSA

30g sundried tomatoes, cut in strips
12 balls *bocconcini* cheese, cut in wedges
2 tbsp olive oil
1 tbsp balsamic vinegar

1 Preheat the oven to 220°C. Slice the French bread into 24 x 1cm thick slices. Mix the olive oil with 1 tbsp of the pesto, the lemon juice and seasoning. Brush both sides of the bread slices with the mixture.

2 In a bowl, mix the minced beef, onion, garlic and remaining pesto, season and shape into 24 evenly sized balls. Thread the meatballs onto the skewers alternating with the bread, so that each person gets 6 meatballs and 6 pieces of bread.

3 Place in the hot oven to bake for 5–6 minutes, until the meatballs are cooked and the bread crisp.

4 Meanwhile, toss the salsa ingredients together and season well with salt and black pepper.

5 Place the polpetti and toast skewers on a dish, and serve with the salsa.

Asian grilled beef in vine leaves

A quality steak mince is vital for these delicate little wraps made from minced steak and hot Thai chillies, and served with a sharp spicy and sour dipping sauce. This is a great dish to prepare on the outdoor charcoal barbecue.

SERVES 4

12 preserved vine leaves in brine, drained
400g steak mince or steak finely chopped
2 shallots, finely chopped
1 hot birdseye Thai chilli, deseeded, finely chopped
2 garlic cloves, crushed
4 lemongrass sticks, outer casing removed, inner finely chopped
1 tsp brown sugar
1 tbsp fish sauce (*nam pla*)
2 tbsp fresh holy basil, chopped
1 tbsp fresh coriander leaves, chopped
3 tbsp sunflower or vegetable oil
12 pre-soaked wooden skewers
lime wedges to garnish

FOR THE DIPPING SAUCE

4 tbsp sweet chilli sauce
4 tbsp fish sauce (*nam pla*)
3 tbsp lime juice
1 garlic clove, crushed

1 Make the dipping sauce. Combine all the ingredients and allow to stand for 1 hour for the flavours to blend.
2 Soak the vine leaves in cold water for 30 minutes, then drain and rinse. Soak again for a further 30 minutes, remove and drain.
3 In a bowl, place the minced steak, shallots, chilli, garlic and lemongrass, and mix well. Add the sugar, fish sauce and herbs and leave to marinate for 30 minutes at room temperature.
4 Ensuring the vine leaves are dry, lay them out on a work surface. Divide the beef mix equally into 12, then fill each leaf with a portion of mince. Roll up the leaves, tucking in the sides, as if making a spring roll.
5 Spear the rolls with a skewer through the centre to hold them together.
6 Heat the barbecue or pan grill until smoking. Brush the beef rolls with oil and place on the grill, turning them once until cooked and lightly charred, about 3–4 minutes each side. Serve with the lime wedges and dipping sauce.

Baked beef and potato frittata

A kitchen mandolin is just the job for slicing the potatoes very thinly for the frittata.

SERVES 4–6

3 tbsp olive oil
500g steak mince
1 small onion, chopped
2 garlic cloves, crushed
1 tsp smoked paprika
400g new potatoes, very thinly sliced
8 free range eggs
5 tbsp full fat milk
2 tbsp freshly chopped flat parsley
1 tsp fresh oregano
salt and freshly cracked black pepper
125g buffalo Mozzarella, grated

1 Preheat the oven to 180°C. Heat a large non-stick frying pan with 1 tbsp of the oil and, when hot, add the steak mince, onion, garlic and paprika and cook for 10–12 minutes breaking up the mince until it is golden and well browned all over. Drain off any excess fat and place the mince on one side.

2 Return the frying pan to the heat, add the remaining oil and cook the potatoes until golden brown, turning them regularly.

3 Return the mince to the pan of potatoes and cook for a further 2–3 minutes.

4 In a bowl, mix the eggs, milk, parsley, oregano and season to taste.

5 Add the cheese to the pan, mix, then stir the pan contents into the bowl with the egg mix. Stir together.

6 Transfer the mix to a large ovenproof casserole and bake for 20–25 minutes or until the eggs are set. Allow to cool slightly before cutting into wedges; serve with crusty bread and a mixed green salad.

Breakfast steak hash with fried egg and black-bean salsa

When it comes to great breakfasts, no one betters the Americans: they love to start the day with a hearty breakfast that sees you through to lunch and well beyond. This is a dish I always prepare when a bowl of cereal just won't do!

SERVES 4
Black-bean salsa (see page 142)
5 tbsp sunflower oil
400g mignon steak, cut in thin strips
½ avocado, stoned, chopped
50g grated Cheddar cheese
4 free range eggs

FOR THE HASH POTATOES
300g cooked potatoes, crushed
2 egg yolks
1 tbsp plain flour
salt and freshly cracked black pepper

1. Make the black-bean salsa (see page 142).
2. Make the hash pototoes. In a bowl, mix the crushed potatoes with the egg yolks and flour, and season with salt and pepper. Mould into 4 small patties, chill for 1 hour.
3. Heat a non-stick frying pan with 1 tbsp of the oil and, when hot, add the potato cakes and cook until golden, about 3–4 minutes on each side. Keep warm.
4. Heat another non-stick frying pan with 1 tbsp of the oil and, when very hot, season the beef with salt and pepper and add to the pan. Fry quickly until sealed and golden all over, then remove from the heat, add the avocado and cheese to the pan, and stir together until the beef is bound in the cheese.
5. In another pan fry the eggs to your preference using the remaining oil.
6. Arrange a potato cake on each serving plate and top with some beef mixture. Top the beef with a fried egg and spoon some of the black-bean salsa over. Serve immediately.

Spicy beef noodles with fennel seeds and Indonesian soy sauce

This dish is one of those dishes you know always delivers – it is extremely tasty and prepared in as long as it takes to cook the noodles.

SERVES 4

2 tbsp *ketjap manis* (Indonesian soy sauce)

1 tbsp sesame oil

2 tbsp dry sherry

2 tsp cornflour

2 garlic cloves, crushed

650g rump steak, thinly sliced

2 tbsp sunflower oil

450g hokkien noodles

175g shiitake mushrooms, sliced

1 red pepper, halved, deseeded, cut into long strips

2.5cm piece root ginger, thinly sliced

1 small green chilli, thinly sliced

1 tsp fennel seeds

1 In a bowl, combine the *ketjap manis*, sesame oil, sherry, cornflour and garlic. Add the beef strips and leave for 10 minutes to marinate. Drain the beef and reserve the marinade.

2 Heat the oil in a wok or large frying pan until smoking. Cook the egg noodles according to the package instructions. Drain well and set the noodles aside.

3 Add the beef to the wok, stir fry for 2–3 minutes, remove and drain.

4 Return the wok to the heat, add the mushrooms, red pepper, ginger, chilli and fennel seeds, and stir fry for 2–3 minutes.

5 Return the beef to the wok, add the reserved marinade and stir fry for 1 more minute. Finally, add the noodles, toss everything together and serve immediately.

Pastrami-style steak burger with rocket, sauerkraut-mayo slaw

Whether it is a plain grilled steak or a burger it is vitally important to use good quality meat. This burger is based on New York's famous deli speciality: pastrami, served on rye bread with sauerkraut stacked higher than the Empire State Building! Here is a burger on this theme; I've used rump steak but any good steak would do the job perfectly.

SERVES 4

FOR THE BURGERS

600g rump steak, well trimmed, chilled

2 shallots, finely chopped

2 tbsp fresh coriander

1 tbsp molasses or black treacle

1 tsp sugar

1 tsp ground coriander

½ tsp smoked paprika

¼ tsp cayenne pepper

pinch of allspice

salt and freshly cracked black pepper

olive oil

4 sesame-seed burger baps, halved

4 slices tomato

handful of small rocket leaves

FOR THE SAUERKRAUT SLAW

750g cooked sauerkraut, drained and chopped

1 carrot, finely shredded

1 red onion, finely shredded

100ml good quality mayonnaise

2 tbsp tomato ketchup

½ tsp caraway seeds

½ tsp Dijon mustard

1 In a large bowl mix all the ingredients for the burgers and chill for up to 1 hour.

2 Shape into 4 evenly sized burgers, brush with a little olive oil and grill on a hot pan or grill, or barbecue over a moderate heat, for 4–5 minutes each side until cooked.

3 For the slaw, mix all the ingredients together in a large bowl and season to taste.

4 Toast the baps and top the bap bases with a heap of the sauerkraut slaw. Place the burgers on top, add a slice of tomato and some rocket leaves, close the top of the bap and serve.

Marinades

A marinade is a liquid that flavours and helps tenderise fish or, more usually, meat as it permeates the flesh. It consists of wine, oil or vinegar, or yoghurt with added herbs or spices. A marinade can also be based on raw fruit juices, including pineapple or papaya, as well as the more familiar lemon or lime. The marinades below are excellent for simple grilled steak. The recipes within the book that use marinades have details given in the appropriate recipe.

Zesty lemon mustard marinade

4 tbsp vegetable oil
2 tbsp white wine vinegar
2 garlic cloves, crushed
1 tsp Dijon mustard
juice of 1 lemon
zest of ¼ lemon

Combine all the ingredients in a bowl. Use to marinate steak for 4 hours or overnight, covered, in the fridge.

Red wine, garlic and herb marinade

150ml good quality red wine
2 tbsp balsamic vinegar
2 tbsp olive oil
2 garlic cloves, crushed
1 tbsp mixed chopped fresh herbs (e.g. rosemary and thyme)

Combine all the ingredients and marinate the steak for 4 hours (but no longer than 8 hours) before cooking.

Yoghurt marinade

125ml natural Greek yoghurt
juice of ½ lemon
1 tbsp tomato juice
1 tsp paprika
1 tsp ground cumin
pinch of sugar
salt and freshly cracked black pepper

Combine all the ingredients in a bowl, add the steak, and leave to marinate for 30 minutes before cooking.

Spicy Asian marinade

4 tbsp olive oil
1 tbsp soy sauce
1 tbsp fish sauce (*nam pla*)
juice of 1 lemon
5cm piece root ginger, grated
2 garlic cloves, crushed
½ tsp cracked black peppercorns

Combine all the ingredients; leave the steak in the marinade for up to 2 hours at room temperature.

Top: Ginger–garlic baste
Left: Honey–mustard baste
Right: Miso–soy baste

Bastes

Bastes – often known as glazes – are brushed onto steaks and roasts as they cook which boosts the flavour and seals in the juices. They generally consist of ingredients with a high sugar content that acts as a caramelisation on the meat forming a rather sticky coating. Continuous basting produces layers of caramelised flavours.

Store bought sauces also make great bastes – hoisin sauce, plum sauce, barbecue sauce, sweet chilli sauce, all work well and are easily available. Below are my favourite bastes for steaks and roasts.

Honey–mustard baste

4 tbsp olive oil
1 tbsp Dijon mustard
1 tbsp honey
1 tbsp sesame oil
2.5cm piece root ginger, grated
2 garlic cloves, crushed
juice of ¼ lemon

Combine all the ingredients in a bowl, leave to infuse for 30 minutes before use.

Tamarind–ketchup baste

100ml tamarind paste
2 tbsp fish sauce (*nam pla*)
2 tbsp soy sauce
2 tbsp rice wine vinegar
2 tbsp brown sugar
2 garlic cloves, crushed
½ tsp dried chilli flakes

Heat the tamarind paste with 4 tbsp water and bring to the boil. Add the remaining ingredients, cook for 1 minute. Allow to cool before use.

Thai barbecue baste

100ml coconut milk
1 tbsp Thai curry paste
4 tbsp soy sauce
2 tbsp olive oil
1 tbsp brown sugar
2.5cm piece root ginger, grated
1 garlic clove, crushed
pinch of turmeric

Heat the coconut milk and curry paste in a pan and simmer for 5 minutes. Cool. Place in a blender with the remaining ingredients, and whiz to a smooth paste ready for use.

Miso–soy baste

2 tbsp soy sauce
2 tbsp apricot jam
2 tbsp brown sugar
1 tbsp white miso paste
½ tsp wasabi paste

Blend all the ingredients to a paste in a blender with 100ml water, ready for use.

Ginger–garlic baste

5cm piece root ginger, grated
6 tbsp olive oil
2 garlic cloves, crushed
salt and freshly cracked black pepper

Place the ginger, olive oil and garlic in a blender and whiz to a paste; season to taste.

Rubs

You may not be so familiar with the use of 'rubs' in cooking – they are used more in America than here in Britain. Rubs are a dry, intensely flavourful alternative to marinades. They are a combination of herbs, usually dried, spices and seasonings blended together and applied to the exterior surface of the meat, just before grilling or roasting. This creates an almost smoky aroma and, forming a crusty coating on the outside, it helps retain the sealed in juices. Simply mix all the ingredients together for each rub and use for your favourite steak.

North African rub

2 tsp ground cumin
2 tsp ground coriander
¼ tsp paprika
1 tsp garlic powder
¼ tsp chilli powder
pinch of turmeric
salt and freshly cracked black pepper

Kitchen Tabasco rub

20g dried porcini mushrooms, ground
  to powder
1 tsp dried thyme
½ tsp dried rosemary
½ tsp garlic powder

Cuban rub

2 tbsp finely ground light-roast coffee
2 tbsp brown sugar
1 tsp dried sage
1 tsp freshly cracked black pepper
½ tsp powdered garlic
pinch of cinnamon
pinch of ground ginger

Five-spice rub

1 tbsp ground cumin
1 tsp ground allspice
1 tsp curry powder
1 tsp ground cinnamon
½ tsp garlic powder
salt and freshly cracked black pepper

Mediterranean rub

1 tbsp ground cumin
1 tsp brown sugar
½ tsp dried tarragon
½ tsp dried oregano
¼ dry mustard powder
salt and freshly cracked black pepper
zest of 1 orange

Left: Béarnaise sauce
Right: Choron variation

Warm butter sauces

For me there is nothing like a good steak with béarnaise sauce – it needs nothing else.

Béarnaise sauce

For me, béarnaise sauce is the ultimate classic steak sauce, fantastic served with plain grilled or roasted beef – a real treat at any time.

30ml tarragon or white wine vinegar
2 tbsp chopped fresh tarragon, retaining the stalks
2 shallots chopped
8 whole peppercorns, lightly cracked
4 egg yolks
250g melted butter, warm
juice of ½ lemon
2 tbsp chopped fresh chervil
salt and freshly cracked black pepper

• Place the vinegar, tarragon stalks, shallots and peppercorns in a small pan, reduce by half over a low heat. Cool then strain into a heatproof bowl. Add the egg yolks and 30ml cold water and whisk together.
• Place the bowl over a pan of simmering water, ensuring the bowl does not touch the water itself. Whisk the mixture until it becomes thick and pale in colour.
• Remove the bowl from the heat and set on tea cloth to hold it steady. Gradually whisk in the warm butter, a little at a time, allowing each addition to thicken and emulsify, until the sauce is thick and glossy.
• Stir in the lemon juice, chopped tarragon and chervil, season to taste and serve.

Variations

CHORON – Add 1 tsp of tomato purée (preferably fresh) to the basic béarnaise sauce.
BALSAMIC – Simply replace half the vinegar in the recipe with balsamic vinegar, then add 1 tbsp more to the finished sauce.
HORSERADISH – Stir 2 tbsp horseradish relish into the basic sauce.
MUSTARD – Add 1 tbsp Dijon mustard to the finished sauce.
OLIVE – See page 12.

Mayonnaise-based sauces

Mayonnaise-based sauces make great sauces to serve with steak, whether plain or made in a variety of flavours with the addition of a few ingredients. For the best results when making mayonnaise ensure all the ingredients are at room temperature.

Basic mayonnaise

2 egg yolks
1 tsp Dijon mustard
1 tsp white wine vinegar
pinch of salt
250ml sunflower or canola oil
2 tsp lemon juice
freshly cracked black pepper

Place the egg yolks, mustard and vinegar in a bowl, and add a pinch of salt. Pour in the oil slowly, at a gradual drizzle, whisking all the time until the mixture thickens. When all the oil has been amalgamated, stir in the lemon juice. Season to taste, ready to serve.

Variations

AIOLI SAUCE – Add 2 crushed garlic cloves to the egg yolks and mustard, then continue as for the basic mayonnaise.
SUNDRIED TOMATO AIOLI – In a blender, whiz 50g sundried tomatoes in oil with 1 crushed garlic clove and a pinch of cayenne pepper. Stir into the basic mayonnaise and season to taste.
PESTO MAYONNAISE – Add 3 tbsp of good quality pesto into the basic mayonnaise, season to taste and serve.
HERB MUSTARD MAYONNAISE – Add 1 tsp Dijon mustard, 1 tsp eacj chopped fresh marjoram and thyme, and a pinch of ground aniseed to the basic mayonnaise.

Cold butters

Cold butters are one of the simplest forms of sauce available to any cook. In all the recipes below, the flavoured butter should be wrapped in greaseproof paper or foil in a bonbon roll and frozen until needed or refrigerated if using soon after making. Cut into slices, it forms a quick sauce for any steak.

Maître d'hôtel or herb butter

150g unsalted butter, softened
1 tbsp chopped fresh tarragon
1 tbsp chopped fresh chives
1 tbsp chopped fresh chervil
1 tbsp chopped fresh Italian flat-leaf
 parsley
salt and freshly cracked black pepper

Mix the butter in a bowl with the herbs and season to taste. Roll and chill ready for use.

Mustard and tarragon butter

150g unsalted butter, softened
2 tbsp chopped fresh tarragon
2 tsp Dijon mustard

Mix all the ingredients in a bowl until amalgamated, roll and chill ready for use.

Garlic and herb butter

150g unsalted butter, softened
4 garlic cloves
2 tbsp mixed chopped fresh herbs (e.g
 Italian flat-leaf parsley, chervil, chives)
juice of ¼ lemon
salt and freshly cracked black pepper
2 tbsp olive oil

In a blender, whiz together the butter, garlic and herbs. Remove to a bowl, season to taste with the lemon juice, salt and pepper, then beat in the olive oil until smooth. Roll and chill ready for use.

Roquefort butter

150g unsalted butter, softened
50g Roquefort cheese, crumbled
1 tsp Dijon mustard
½ tsp cognac
salt and freshly cracked black pepper

Mix all the ingredients in a bowl and beat until smooth; season to taste, roll and chill ready for use.

Anchovy and lemon–olive butter

150g unsalted butter softened
15 anchovy fillets, rinsed, dried, chopped
10 black olives, pitted
freshly cracked black pepper
zest of ¼ lemon
2 tbsp olive oil

Place the butter, anchovies and olives into a blender, pulse process until smooth. Transfer to a bowl, season with pepper, add the lemon zest, then beat in the olive oil until smooth. Roll and chill ready for use.

Maître d'hôtel
or herb butter

Café de Paris butter

2 tbsp tomato ketchup
1 shallot, finely chopped
1 tbsp chopped fresh chives
1 tsp Dijon mustard
1 tsp chopped fresh tarragon
1 tsp cognac
1 tsp Worcester sauce
½ tsp chopped capers
2 anchovy fillets
pinch of paprika
salt and freshly cracked black pepper
150g unsalted butter, softened

Place all the ingredients except the butter in a bowl, leave the mixture to stand for 24 hours in a warm place to allow the flavours to infuse. Beat the mix into the softened butter, then roll and chill ready for use.

Montpellier butter

15g watercress, leaves only
15g spinach leaves
15g fresh picked chervil
150g unsalted butter, softened
2 small gherkins
1 anchovy fillet
1 garlic clove, crushed
1 tsp capers
½ tsp Dijon mustard
juice of ¼ lemon
2 tbsp olive oil

Blanch the watercress, spinach and chervil quickly in a small pan of boiling water, then refresh them in a colander under cold running water. Squeeze and dry in a cloth. Place the butter in a blender, add the herbs and remaining ingredients except the oil, pulse process until smooth. Remove, beat in the olive oil, roll and chill ready for use.

Porcini butter

10g dried porcini mushrooms
150g unsalted butter
2 tbsp chopped fresh chives
1 small garlic clove, crushed
½ tsp lemon juice
salt and freshly cracked black pepper

Place the porcini in a small pan, cover with 150ml water, bring to the boil, reduce the heat and simmer for 20 minutes. Remove the mushrooms, reserve the liquid. Return the liquid to the pan and boil until it reduces to 2 tbsp of a mushroom syrup. Dry the mushrooms in a cloth and chop. Place in a bowl, add the butter, mushroom syrup, chives, garlic and lemon juice; season to taste. Roll and chill ready for use.

Tapenade butter

150g unsalted butter, softened
50g black olives, pitted and chopped
2 tsp olive oil
1 garlic clove, crushed
1 small anchovy fillet, chopped
freshly cracked black pepper

Place the butter in a blender with the other ingredients and pulse whiz to a purée quickly. Roll and chill ready for use.

Watercress and almond butter

150g unsalted butter, softened
40g toasted almonds, chopped
25g watercress, leaves only
1 garlic clove, crushed
juice of ¼ lemon
salt and freshly cracked black pepper

Mix all the ingredients in a bowl until amalgamated, roll and chill ready for use.

Red wine butter

150ml red wine
50ml well-flavoured beef stock
1 tsp red wine vinegar
2 shallots, finely chopped
sprig of fresh thyme
1 tbsp redcurrant jelly
150g unsalted butter, softened
salt and freshly cracked black pepper
2 tbsp olive oil

In a pan place the red wine, stock, vinegar, shallots and thyme and boil until reduced by half in volume. Strain, and add the redcurrant jelly, dissolving it in the wine mixture.
When cold, mix with the butter, season to taste, then beat in the olive oil until smooth. Roll and chill ready for use.

Top left: Café de Paris butter
Top right: Montepellier butter
Centre: Watercress and almond butter
Bottom left: Porcini butter
Bottom right: Tapenade butter

Other great steak sauces

Here are some of my favourite steak sauces that just add that final touch of luxury to a dish, most based on the foundation of traditional French sauce making techniques.

Sauce chasseur

Bordelaise (MAKES 450ML)

25g unsalted butter, chilled, cut into small
  pieces
2 shallots, finely chopped
6 crushed black peppercorns
1 sprig of fresh thyme
1 small bay leaf
300ml good quality red wine
150ml thickened beef stock (see page 141)
salt

• Heat 10g of the butter in a pan and add
the shallots and peppercorns. Add the thyme
and bay leaf and pour 250ml of the red wine
into the pan. Bring to the boil and boil
vigorously until the wine has reduced by two
thirds in volume.

• Add the stock and cook for 15 minutes,
then strain, pressing down on the strainer
to extract the flavour from the shallots .
Return to the boil, add the remaining red
wine, season to taste, stir in the remaining
butter and serve.

Diable (MAKES 450ML)

25g unsalted butter, chilled, cut into small
  pieces
2 shallots, finely chopped
12 crushed black peppercorns
1 sprig of thyme
1 small bay leaf
150ml dry white wine
2 tbsp wine vinegar
300ml thickened beef stock (see page 141)
½ tsp Worcester sauce
pinch of cayenne pepper
salt and freshly cracked black pepper

• Heat 10g of the butter in a small pan, add
the shallots and peppercorns and cook for
1 minute. Add the thyme, bay leaf, pour in
the wine and wine vinegar, and boil rapidly
to reduce by half in volume.

• Add the beef stock, Worcester sauce,
cayenne and simmer for 10 minutes. Strain
the sauce, then reheat, season to taste, stir
in the remaining butter and serve.

Chasseur (MAKES 450ML)

25g unsalted butter, chilled, cut into small
  pieces
2 shallots, finely chopped
100g button mushrooms
100ml dry white wine
1 tbsp tarragon vinegar
1 tbsp cognac
300ml thickened beef stock (see page 141)
400g canned tomatoes, finely chopped
1 tbsp tomato purée
2 tbsp mixed chopped fresh herbs (e.g.
  tarragon, Italian flat-leaf parsley)
salt and freshly cracked black pepper

Heat 10g of the butter in a pan, add the
shallots, cook until tender. Add the
mushrooms, cook for 5 minutes. Pour the
white wine, vinegar and cognac over and boil
for 5 minutes. Add the beef stock, tomatoes
and tomato purée. Simmer for 10–15
minutes, then add the herbs. Remove from
the heat, stir in remaining butter, season to
taste and serve.

Left: Madeira sauce   Right: Sauce Grand Veneur

Robert (MAKES 400ML)

25g unsalted butter chilled, cut into small
  pieces
1 small onion, finely chopped
100ml dry white wine
2 tbsp white wine vinegar
300ml thickened beef stock (see
  opposite)
3 tsp Dijon mustard
salt and freshly cracked black pepper

· Heat 10g of the butter in a small pan,
add the onion and cook over a low heat for
8–10 minutes until cooked but not
coloured. Pour in the wine and wine vinegar,
and reduce by half in volume.

· Pour in the stock, cook for 15 minutes,
then strain, pressing down on the onions to
extract maximum flavour. Reheat, add the
mustard, the remaining butter, season to
taste then serve.

Chateaubriand (MAKES 400ML)

15g unsalted butter, chilled, cut into
  small pieces
2 shallots, finely chopped
75g flat mushrooms, roughly chopped
1 sprig of fresh thyme
1 small bay leaf
100ml dry white wine
300ml thickened beef stock (see opposite)
75g prepared herb butter (maître d'hôtel)
  (see page 134)
1 tbsp chopped fresh tarragon
salt and freshly cracked black pepper

· Heat the butter in a small pan, add the
shallots and mushrooms, and cook for
5–6 minutes.

· Add the thyme, bay leaf, pour the wine
over and cook for 5 minutes. Add the beef
stock, cook for 15 minutes, then strain it
thoroughly.

· Reheat the sauce. Add the prepared herb
butter, the chopped tarragon, season to taste
and serve.

Madeira sauce

One of the classic steak sauces, full
of flavour and a complete taste.

300ml thickened beef stock (see opposite)
100ml Madeira wine
15g unsalted butter, chilled, cut into small
  pieces
salt and freshly cracked black pepper

Bring the stock and Madeira to the boil,
simmer for 10 minutes. Whisk in the chilled
butter, season and serve.

Roquefort

50g unsalted butter
2 shallots
4 tbsp dry white wine
1 tbsp cognac
200ml thickened beef stock (see opposite)
150ml double cream
50g whole blanched almonds
75g Roquefort cheese
salt and freshly cracked black pepper

Heat 10g of the butter in a small pan, add
the shallots and cook for 5 minutes until
softened. Pour in the white wine and cognac
and bring to the boil. Add the stock and boil
for 10 minutes. Add the cream, mix well and
simmer for a further 5 minutes. Place the
almonds, remaining butter and the cheese in
a blender and process to a smooth paste.
Whisk paste into the sauce, remove from the
heat and strain. Season to taste and serve.

Quick barbecue sauce

2 tbsp vegetable oil
1 onion, finely chopped
1 garlic clove, crushed
juice of 1 lemon
100g brown sugar
4 tbsp red wine vinegar
125ml tomato ketchup
1 tbsp Worcester sauce
2 tbsp Mexican style hot chilli sauce or
  ½ tsp Tabasco
½ tsp Dijon mustard
salt and freshly cracked black pepper

Heat the oil in a frying pan, add the onion
and garlic, and cook until soft and lightly
browned for 5 minutes. Add lemon juice,
sugar, vinegar, ketchup, Worcester sauce, hot
chilli sauce and mustard. Simmer together
for 8–10 minutes to allow the flavours to
infuse. Adjust the seasoning, ready to serve.

Lyonnaise

Steak and onions makes a great match, as here, in a piquant sauce.

25g unsalted butter, chilled, cut into small
  pieces
2 onions, halved, thinly sliced
150ml dry white wine
100ml white wine vinegar
300ml thickened beef stock (see below)
salt and freshly cracked black pepper

Heat 10g of the butter in a pan, add the onions and fry until lightly golden and tender. Pour in the wine and vinegar and reduce by half. Add the stock and simmer for 15 minutes. Season, stir in the remaining butter and serve.

Sauce Grand Veneur

This sauce is traditionally served with venison, but it is impressive with steak marinaded in red wine.

150ml good quality red wine
2 tbsp cognac
10 crushed black peppercorns
2 shallots, finely chopped
175ml thickened beef stock (see below)
100ml double cream
2 tbsp redcurrant jelly
10g unsalted butter
1 tsp Worcester sauce
salt

Heat the red wine, cognac, peppercorns and shallots in a pan, bring to the boil and reduce by half. Add the stock and cream, return to the boil, simmer for 10 minutes, then strain. Whisk in the redcurrant jelly, butter and Worcester sauce. Season and serve.

Dijonnaise

4 tbsp white wine
4 tbsp port
2 small shallots, chopped
200ml thickened beef stock (see below)
100ml double cream
15g unsalted butter
2 tbsp Dijon mustard
salt and freshly cracked black pepper

Place the wine, port and shallots in a pan and bring to the boil. Add the stock and boil for 10 minutes. Add the cream and simmer for a further 5 minutes. Whisk the butter into the sauce, add the mustard, season to taste and serve.

Horseradish sauce

1 tbsp white wine vinegar
juice of ¼ lemon
75g fresh white breadcrumbs
½ tsp Dijon mustard
125ml lightly whipped double cream
2 tbsp freshly grated horseradish
pinch of sugar
salt and freshly cracked black pepper

In a bowl, mix the vinegar, lemon juice, breadcrumbs and mustard and leave to stand for 30 minutes. Fold in the cream, horseradish and sugar, season to taste and serve.

Beef stock (MAKES 2.5 LITRES)

As you will discover throughout the book, the outcome of each recipe often relies on the base stock. This is a simple recipe for making your own beef stock, which can be made and then frozen if necessary.

2kg beef bones, chopped
2 unpeeled onions, quartered
2 large carrots, quartered
1 stick celery, chopped
4 garlic cloves, unpeeled
½ tsp tomato purée
1 tsp black peppercorns
2 sprigs of thyme
1 bay leaf

• Preheat the oven to 230°C. Place the bones in a large roasting pan and roast in the oven until well browned, about 1½ hours. Remove the bones and place in a large saucepan or stockpot.
• Add the onions, carrots, celery, garlic and tomato purée to the roasting pan, return the pan to the oven and cook until the vegetables are browned, almost charred, about 40 minutes, stirring regularly to prevent them sticking.
• Add the vegetables to the pan with the bones, and add the peppercorns and herbs. Cover with 5 litres of water, bring to the boil, slowly, skimming it often.
• Simmer gently for 3 hours, adding more water to cover if necessary and skimming it regularly. Strain through a fine strainer and chill well. Once chilled, skim off any fat with a spoon before use.

Thickened beef stock

This forms the basis of many of the great classic steak sauces: it is quick and simple to make.

2 tbsp arrowroot or fécule (potato flour)
100ml Madeira wine
500ml stock
salt and freshly cracked black pepper

Mixed the arrowroot and Madeira together; bring the stock to the boil then whisk the arrowroot mixture into it. Return to the boil, strain and season to taste, ready for use.

My favourite salsas for steaks

Salsas make great condiments to accompany steaks, especially when you are looking for something quick and simple to prepare. Here is a small selection of my particular favourites which, when served with any good steak, will enhance it and impact on the overall taste experience.

Five-onion salsa

This salsa is also good with beef burgers.

4 spring onions, roughly chopped
1 red onion, roughly diced
2 shallots, halved, thinly sliced
small bunch of fresh chives, snipped
1 garlic clove, thinly sliced
1 tbsp maple syrup
⅛ tsp dried chilli flakes

Place all the ingredients in a bowl, leave to marinate at room temperature for 30 minutes before use. This salsa must be prepared and used immediately; it cannot be refrigerated and used later.

Provençale salsa

50g sunblush tomatoes in oil
4 tbsp olive oil
2 tbsp chopped black olives
1 tbsp chopped fresh Italian flat-leaf
  parsley
1 tbsp superfine capers, rinsed
1 tbsp red wine vinegar
2 garlic cloves, crushed
1 anchovy fillet, chopped
1 tsp maple syrup
salt and freshly cracked black pepper

Cut the tomatoes in half, place in a bowl with the remaining ingredients and season to taste. Toss together and leave to infuse for 30 minutes. Use immediately or refrigerate until needed.

Creole-style salsa

1 red pepper, deseeded, cut into 1cm dice
100g fresh mango, cut into 1cm dice
1 red onion, cut into small dice
4 tbsp chopped fresh coriander
2 tbsp maple syrup
juice of 1 lemon
juice of 2 limes
pinch of dried chilli flakes
salt and freshly cracked black pepper

Mix all the ingredients together in a bowl and season to taste. Leave to infuse for 30 minutes before use.

Asian tomato salsa

2 yellow tomatoes, cut into 1cm dice
2 plum tomatoes, cut into 1cm dice
2 shallots, halved, thinly sliced
2 tbsp rice wine vinegar
2 tbsp chopped fresh coriander
1.5cm piece root ginger, finely chopped
1 tsp sugar
1 tsp fish sauce (*nam pla*)
salt and freshly cracked black pepper

Mix all the ingredients together in a bowl and season to taste. Leave to infuse for 30 minutes before use.

Spicy chilli salsa

4 tbsp red wine vinegar
4 tbsp extra virgin olive oil
salt and freshly cracked black pepper
3 large ripe tomatoes, diced
4 tbsp chopped fresh cilantro
1 small red onion, peeled, halved and
  thinly sliced
1 serrano chilli, finely chopped
2 tsp chipotle pepper purée
2 tsp honey

Whisk together the vinegar, oil, salt and pepper in a medium bowl. Add the remaining ingredients and toss to combine. Leave to infuse for 30 minutes before use.

Blood orange and avocado salsa

1 avocado, halved, stoned and diced
2 blood oranges
1 red onion, finely chopped
2 spring onions, finely shredded
juice of 2 limes
little chopped fresh tarragon and coriander

Place the avocado in a bowl, add the orange segments and juice, the onion, spring onions and lime juice. Add the fresh herbs, mix well and chill until needed.

Black-bean salsa

2 tomatoes, blanched, deseeded, diced
½ red pepper, cut into 5mm dice
100g cooked or canned black beans
1 red onion, chopped
1 small red chilli, deseeded, finely chopped
1 tbsp chopped fresh coriander
½ tbsp maple syrup
juice of 1 lime

Mix the ingredients together in a bowl, leave to infuse for 1 hour.

Cranberry–beetroot relish

225g frozen cranberries
4 tbsp caster sugar
1 Granny Smith apple, peeled, cored, grated
1 tsp finely chopped stem ginger
2 tbsp white wine vinegar
juice and zest of 1 orange
2 large pickled beetroots, cut into wedges

Place all he ingredients except the beetroots in a pan with 150ml water. Bring to the boil and simmer until thickened. Cool, then add beetroots, ready for use.

Top left: Five-onion salsa   Right: Creole-style salsa   Bottom left: Provençale salsa

Acknowledgements

To Jacqui and Kate of Jacqui Small publishers for giving me the opportunity to express my thoughts on steak cookery. Once again, it has been a real pleasure working with you – you have, as always, been both inspirational and supportive.

The beautiful look and content of the book is due to the enthusiasm and professionalism of the following people:

Good friend Linda Tubby, food stylist, for cooking the recipes for the book's photography and Peter Cassidy, photographer: I thank them both for bringing the dishes to life so artfully. To Lawrence Morton, art director, and Roisin Nield, prop stylist, for brilliantly conveying the very soul and feel I wanted for this book. To Madeline Weston, a truly professional editor, I thank you for your patience, understanding and for keeping the whole project on course at all times. To Jane Middleton, for her help in the early stages of manuscripts, from the time of the book's conception. To Lara King: I do not know what I would do without you; your speed, efficiency and organisation never fail to amaze me. A thank-you to my chefs, especially Paolo Genuino, who was especially helpful with recipe testing for the book.

A special thank-you to Managing Director Gerry Wensley and John Jenkins of the butchers Fairfax Meadows, for their kind generosity and support providing the many cuts of meat required for the photography. I also thank you for supplying top quality meat for me to use on a daily basis at the hotel for our exacting clientele to enjoy!

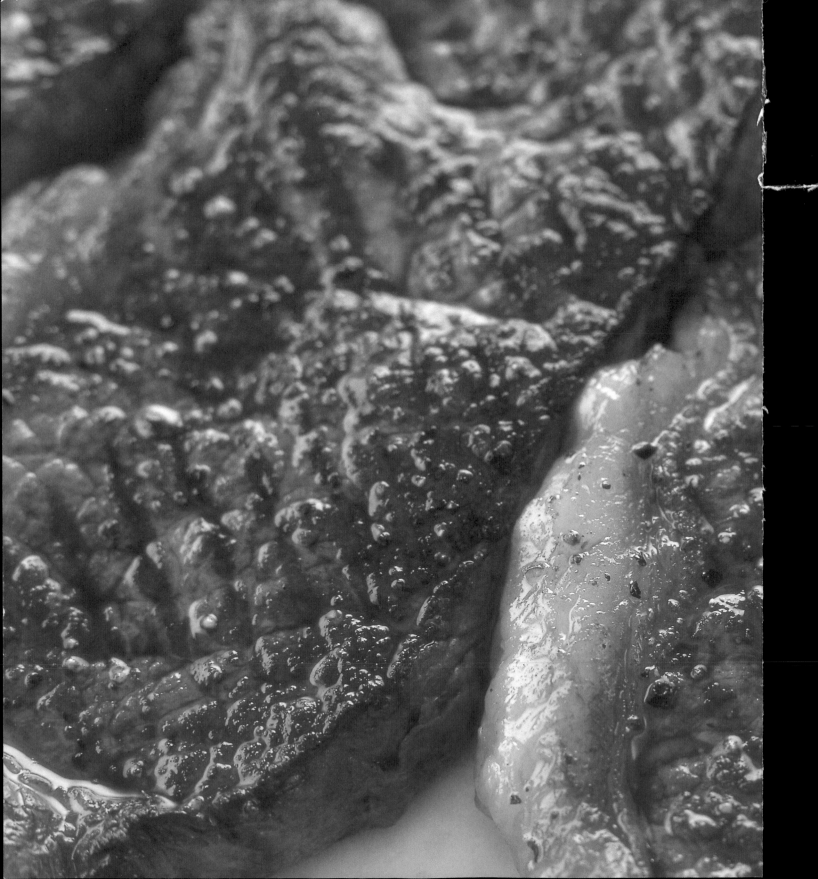